# TWO FERRIES OUT

## GROWING UP ON BRIER ISLAND

## Ben Robicheau

© 2021 Ben Robicheau

All rights reserved. No part of this book may be reproduced or transmitted in any form or by any means, electronic or mechanical, including photocopying, or by any information storage or retrieval system, without permission in writing from the publisher.

Cover image: Rebekah Wetmore, from an image by Ben Robicheau
Other images courtesy of Amy Tudor, Dini Baker, John Thurber, Clayton Titus, Laura Titus, and Frits Verburgh.
Editor: Andrew Wetmore

ISBN: 978-1-990187-13-1

First edition June, 2021

397 Parker Mountain Road
Granville Ferry, NS   B0S 1A0

moosehousepress.com
info@moosehousepress.com

We live and work in Mi'kma'ki, the ancestral and unceded territory of the Mi'kmaq People. This territory is covered by the "Treaties of Peace and Friendship" which Mi'kmaq and Wolastoqiyik (Maliseet) People first signed with the British Crown in 1725. The treaties did not deal with surrender of lands and resources but in fact recognized Mi'kmaq and Wolastoqiyik (Maliseet) title and established the rules for what was to be an ongoing relationship between nations. We are all Treaty people.

This book is dedicated to Brier Island and to my grandchildren, who I hope will have the opportunity to experience some of the Island the way I did.

# Contents

1: Memories of Westport..................................9
2: Geology........................................................11
3: Gull Rock Farm..........................................15
4: Meeting Mom..............................................23
5: This old house.............................................31
6: How the Department of Immigration saved my life..................................................................39
7: Borrowed boats and broken bones............47
8: The Little Store...........................................55
9: In the comic book corner...........................63
10: Go play outside........................................69
11: Breastwork blues......................................77
12: A spring bike ride....................................89
13: Going downhill........................................99
14: Movie night.............................................107
15: TV time....................................................115
16: Family day..............................................123
17: California dreamin'................................131
18: The working life.....................................139
19: The Robicheaus go to Expo 67.............151
20: A trip to the New England states.........155
21: A woman ahead of her time..................171
22: Ace – trial by fire..................................179
23: Iron Will.................................................187
24: Hello, Elsie.............................................195
25: Big dogs and dental work.....................201
26: Roadwork...............................................207
27: Westport Academy.................................215
28: The Great Christmas Tree Hunt...........223
29: The little house out back.......................229
30: Island Christmas traditions..................235

31: Holiday shopping.................................241
32: Hand-made in Westport.......................249
33: Turkey, lobster, and pie—oh, my!...................257
34: Halloween in Westport.......................265
35: Lost at sea on Christmas Eve..........................273
36: Fogged in....................................283
37: Hurricane season.............................289
38: Smoke on the water...........................297
39: Rock music....................................305
40: On the road with Murf the Surf.......................309
41: Strawberry fields forever................................317
42: A whale of a tale.............................325
43: Eastward bound.............................333
44: On being an Islander.........................341
45: Two ferries out................................349
Acknowledgements...............................359
About the author..................................361

**Ben Robicheau**

# 1: Memories of Westport

Ferry boat trip
Little store
Water wells
Fishing wharves
Trawling tubs
Pea Jack
High Knoll
Jim Coggins
Road scrapers
Finnan Haddie
Up the road
Thanks Westport

Ferry slip
Stanley Moore
Dry wells
Long-billed caps
Seining nets
Irishtown
Back to shore
Frankie Buck
Pickup trucks
Codfish tongues
Down the road
Thanks a lot

High tides
Pond Cove
Robicheau's
Saturday night shows
Winter squalls
Harbour whales
Harbour sharks
Fish bones
Ice cold water
Making ice cream
Up the road
Thanks Westport

Low tides
Fishing eels
Baby girls
Seven cent pop
Soaring seagulls
Peters Island
Fairway buoy
Gurrey boat
Summer swims
Vanilla extract
Down the road
Thanks a lot

**Ben Robicheau**

Splitting fish
Grubbing up
Digging clams
Lobster traps
Winter mitts
Winter storms
Putt-putt engines
Going drailing
Old Doc McDonald
Loaded boats
Up the road
Thanks Westport

Drying racks
Jigging squid
Periwinkles
Lobster boats
Winter storms
Men lost at sea
One lung saws
Rip tides
Nellie
Late night work
Down the road
Thanks a lot

Joshua Slocum
Hurricanes
Daniel Kenney
Milking cows
Lester Pugh
Raymond's store
Fishing with Wick
Going to school
First teacher
New Lane
Up the road
Thanks Westport

Western light
Copper mine
Ace
Ferry scows
Stacking hay
Annie Moore
Getting seasick
Tony and Neil
Mr. Fields
Back Road
Down the road
Thanks a lot

by Frits Verburgh

## 2: Geology

Approximately two hundred million years ago, a kilometres-long fissure in the earth's crust allowed a spume of molten lava to squeeze to the surface. As it cooled, it created a mountainous ridge along what eventually would become the Bay of Fundy coast of the province of Nova Scotia.

Today, what we call the North Mountain rises out of the tidal waters of Minas Basin, creating a picturesque geographic anomaly known as Cape Split. From here it marches off in a south-westerly direction, defining Nova Scotia's inner coastline and, for the first hundred kilometres or so, shielding the fertile Annapolis Valley from the ravages of the Bay of Fundy.

At Victoria Beach, some ancient shift in the earth's crust created a break in this ridge of columnar basalt, opening a passageway known as the Digby Gut. The Fundy waters flowing through the Gut flooded the valley behind, creating The Annapolis Basin, an interior harbour that has provided a safe haven to boaters for generations. The effect of the Fundy's ebb and flow on this body of water produces the motive power that turned the turbines farther up the valley at the Annapolis Royal tidal power generating station. The station, which opened in 1984 and was decommissioned in 2021, was one of the first tidal power plants in the world.

The North Mountain picks up again on the Digby side of the Gut, splitting off from the mainland and striking out on its own, driving a long, thin finger out into the Bay of Fundy. Running parallel to the mainland, Digby Neck, as this narrow isthmus is called, separates St. Mary's Bay from its bigger, better-known sister. As the mountain range proceeds, it begins a slow descent back into the sea. From the mainland it presents a long, low profile, alternating between eroded mountain tops and sudden valleys.

At East Ferry, through another fracture known as Petit Passage, the waters flow freely back and forth between the two bays. Across this passage, the mountain range, now greatly diminished, staggers on, down the fifteen-kilometre length of Long Island, to the next and final break in the chain, Grand Passage.

Here, on the other side of this passage, one hundred and ninety kilometres from Cape Split, this six-kilometre-long splinter of weathered and time-worn basalt marks the end of the North Mountain Range. At a small protrusion called Point d'Field, between Big Pond Cove and Hog Yard Cove, the mountain makes its final descent back into the Atlantic. A tidal-covered ledge runs out from Point d'Field to a microscopic speck of barely-above-high-water land known as Green Island, then continues on to a tide-tortured fragment of stone named Gull Rock. Visible only at low tide, Gull Rock stands alone among the waves

## Two Ferries Out

like a tombstone, marking the notorious, barely-submerged, vessel-eating Southwest Ledge, the final visible remnant of the North Mountain Range.

The mountain range now vanishes from human sight. What remains is below the surface of the Atlantic Ocean, its presence known only to a few savvy fishermen who avoid this area, where the waters of the Bay of Fundy and St. Mary's Bay sweep up the submerged mountain sides, meeting at the surface in a strong and dangerous eddy of tides known as "The Rip".

This is where The North Mountain ends.

This is Brier Island.

This is where I grew up.

**Ben Robicheau**

*Pond Cove viewed from Pointe D'Field*

## 3: Gull Rock Farm

The Robicheau family's connection to Brier Island began during the early years of the First World War. At that time, many people on the island were fisher-farmers with a few dairy cows and maybe a team of horses or oxen. To feed these animals through the winter, they turned many of the fields that stretch from behind the houses along the Back Road up to the bottom of the hill to the production of hay.

Due to lack of either time or interest, probably both in some cases, many of these fishermen were disinclined to get involved with more menial agricultural tasks like the harvesting of the hay. Instead they hired young men from the French Shore, on the other side of St. Mary's Bay, to do this work.

That is how my grandfather, Terence, first came to the island, and how he met my grandmother, Albina Ellis—or Biney, as he called her. After a two-year delay while he went off to fight in The Great War, they married in June, 1918.

The ensuing years were tough. In search of affordable accommodations on the island for their growing family, they moved several times, and at one point, rented a whole house for the grand total of a dollar and a half per month.

To support his family, my grandfather worked at a variety of jobs. For a while he was the cook on a rum-runner, a job that ended in an exciting manner, when his ship was deliberately run aground in Scataway Cove to escape a pursuing police boat.

After this abrupt end to his employment, he secured a more respectable position with a New Brunswick fish processor. This new job required that he and his family relocate to be the only residents of a small island off the coast of Grand Manan Island. This job also ended in a sudden and dramatic way, when they were burned out on Christmas Eve. The family of two adults and four kids escaped in a dory in the middle of the night, paddling through sea-ice wearing only the clothes in which they had gone to bed.

After spending some recovery time with relatives in Meteghan, the family returned to Brier Island when Grampy was hired to be the manager of Gull Rock Farm.

If you venture down Gull Rock Road today, you will find that it ends at what was once a large hay field. If you continue straight ahead through the now-overgrown wild grass and clumps of alders, you come upon a bit of a rise just before the land ends at Pointe d'Field. If you stand here facing out to sea, you see in front of you Green Island, and Gull Rock a little further out. Behind you, over your right shoulder, lie Big and Little Pond Coves. Glancing to your left, you can see Hog Yard Cove nearby, and, if it's a clear day, the green smudge of the French Shore in the far distance across St. Mary's Bay

## Two Ferries Out

Where you are standing, is where the big cow barn once stood. Looking around in the overgrown grass and brush near the base of the hill on the inland side, you might still be able to make out the stone remnants of a small farmhouse cellar and, a little beyond that, the circular impression of the old well. Once upon a time, this was Gull Rock Farm; this is where my father came to live with his parents and three sisters when he was a young boy.

Of all the places on the Island, this could well be the most unlikely spot in which to take up homesteading. Dad and his family lived here during the early years of the 1930s. Homes on the Island were wired for electricity and telephones by 1929, but neither of those modern conveniences ever reached Gull Rock Farm.

This is about as far as you can get from town without actually leaving the Island. You're right out on the bitter end of a treeless and unprotected point, exposed to that cold, salt-laden Atlantic Ocean wind as it whips in over the Pond Cove beach and across the open fields. As the salt-stunted trees that border the field can attest, it seems like it would be hard to grow anything at all here, but over the years, several different families braved the elements in a valiant, but ultimately fruitless, battle with Mother Nature to make Gull Rock Farm a success.

Despite the less-than-ideal farming conditions, my grandfather did manage to coax out of the rocky soil a garden that produced potatoes, carrots and turnips, among other things. The garden produced not only enough to feed his own family, but enough extra that he was able to make a little money supplying people in town with fresh vegetables.

Besides the vegetable garden, he also kept a herd of milk cows that he put out to pasture in Big Meadow behind the ponds. To keep these cows and any other farm animals from wandering away, the only road from the farm to town was blocked by what we called "Jackass Gate". The primary, unbreakable rule of Gull Rock Farm was, "Always Close the Gate".

Every weekday, Dad and his three sisters had to make the long walk to school and back. As they left the farm and started up Gull Rock Road towards town, they passed through Jackass Gate. One morning, they noticed that someone had committed the unpardonable sin of leaving the gate open, allowing several cows to wander through. Before they could continue to school, they had to return the cows to the other side of the gate.

Unfortunately, the road was narrow and thickly lined with dense brush, making it impossible to circle around and get in front of the cows, so they tried just walking slowly towards the cows, with the idea of quietly passing through the herd. The cows of course, kept moving away farther up the road. Next, they tried the opposite approach, taking the cows by surprise by suddenly running through them. This resulted in the herd bolting even further along, heading for town at a brisk clip and leaving my

## Two Ferries Out

father and his sisters with no option but to trot along behind.

By the time the village chimneys started coming into view over the crest of the hill, the cows had tired out somewhat and slowed down. Just before the end of the road, where the herd of cows would have spilled out onto the main street of Westport, a clearing finally appeared, providing the kids with an opportunity to skirt the herd, circle around in front, and turn them back.

Now they had to drive the escapees all the way back down the road, make sure the gate was securely closed behind them this time, then walk all the way back to town, for a second time that morning, and then explain to the teacher why they were late.

Chasing cows and growing vegetables were only a couple of the necessary chores in the struggle to make the little farm successful. My grandfather grew his own wheat and tobacco, gathered seaweed off Pond Cove beach to use as fertilizer, hunted ducks, rabbits, and the occasional deer, smoked fish and meat, milked the cows, cut hay, raised chickens and pigs, even trapped eels in Big Pond.

Some of the people who had attempted life on the farm before our family had occasionally made a bit of extra cash by salvaging wreckage from ships that had the bad luck to run across the Southwest Ledge at low tide, or that attempted a short-cut over The Bars between Green Island and Gull Rock.

**Ben Robicheau**

Life on the farm was tough, and probably not too different from that lived by the first settlers on the Island a hundred and fifty years earlier, but my father remembers it with a certain amount of fondness. This was during what would come to be known as The Great Depression. Compared to many in the world, and even some right there on the island, they were not so bad off.

Despite the hardships involved in maintaining an existence on Gull Rock Farm, there are some aspects of life there that my father still recalls with a chuckle. One of these events involved his best friend, Eugene Frost. One day, late in the summer, Genie, as he was known, visited Dad at the farm and the two of them went berry picking. Returning home with a good harvest of wild strawberries, they decided that topping them off with a dollop of fresh cream would make them taste even better.

The farm's well, which was quite large and had a protective shed built over it, doubled as a cooler for milk. The metal cans were immersed in the cold water until they could be shipped by boat to the dairy in Yarmouth.

While scooping some cream off the top of the milk, Genie noticed some of Grampy's tobacco leaves hanging up to dry in the wellhouse rafters, so he reached up and tore off a piece of the raw tobacco.

After enjoying a delicious feed of wild strawberries swimming in a generous helping of rich cream, Genie rolled up the scrap of tobacco leaf and set back to enjoy his homemade cigar. Now, here we have a young boy full of wild berries and heavy cream, and we mix in the strong smoke of home-grown, half-cured tobacco! What could possibly go wrong? Genie only got a few puffs in on his make-shift stogie before the strawberries and cream made a sudden and dramatic reappearance!

To this day, my father still loves the taste of fresh strawberries, but maybe being an unwilling witness to this event is one of the reasons he never became attracted to smoking.

My father, his sisters, and their parents, were the last people to live on Gull Rock Farm. Like the people before them, who for over a hundred years, on and off, had tried to make a go of it on this windswept southernmost point of Brier Island, they did their best to scratch a living from this rugged and unforgiving part of the Island.

But in the end, just as all the others had discovered, it turned out to be far too much work for too little reward. So when a better opportunity came along, Gull Rock Farm was once again abandoned, for what turned out to be the final time.

Within a year of their leaving, the little house burned to the ground. Soon after, the barn met a similar fate. Today, after decades of being blasted by wind and rain and sun, very little tangible evidence remains of those years of hard labour and high hopes. All that exists of the little homestead at the end of the earth is in the memory of my father, the last person who remembers life on Gull Rock farm.

**Ben Robicheau**

*Raymond and Riekie's wedding*

## 4: Meeting Mom

Dad left Gull Rock Farm at the age of thirteen to go to work at Shorecrest Lodge on Grand Manan Island for the princely sum of four dollars a week. From there, he graduated to night manager at a hotel in Saint John, New Brunswick, more than doubling his weekly pay to ten dollars. At the age of fifteen, he left the hospitality industry behind to build mine sweepers on the night shift at Meteghan Shipyards. His next step was to Labrador, where he worked on constructing the Goose Bay airport. After six months, he returned from up north, and in 1941, lied about his age to join the army at the age of sixteen.

After training in England, he landed at Juneau Beach in Normandy in 1944 and joined a rebuilt Second Antitank Regiment which had been nearly wiped out. Fighting through France, Belgium and Germany, he was part of the Allied forces that worked their way through The Netherlands during the winter of 1944-45, pushing the German Army back across the border and liberating Dutch cities, towns and villages.

One of the hardest-fought battles was in and around Nijmegen, a city in eastern Holland right on the Dutch-German border, where a strategically placed bridge across the Waal River was of vital importance to both the retreating German Army and the advancing Allies. When the bombing ended and the people of Nijmegen were finally freed from the Nazi occupation they had been living under since the beginning of the war, they did what they could to thank the soldiers that had risked so much.

One night, a dance was arranged for the troops, and Marie Verburgh's family urged her to attend. Marie's fiancée had recently become a victim of the war and her mother thought a bit of social interaction might help to get her mind on other things. Marie resisted the idea of attending the dance, but finally agreed that she would go if one of her sisters came along. After a bit of persuading, her younger sister Riekie reluctantly agreed to accompany her as long as she didn't have to actually dance with anyone. Riekie knew that Canadian soldiers would be at this dance, and, according to some British soldiers who had been recently billeted in her home, Canadians were all crude, rowdy, backwoodsmen who didn't know how to behave in polite society, and she would be wise to avoid the brutes.

Marie did get into the spirit of things, and while she danced, Riekie tried to fade into the background, turning down offers from several soldiers. The evening was almost over when a tall, dark, and handsome Canadian with a dashing black moustache approached her. This time she said yes, and the couple just had time for a waltz or two before the evening ended. That was how my father met my mother.

Over the following weeks and months, there were many visits to the Verburgh home at 43 Dobbelmannweg. The Verburgh family quickly discovered that Canadians were much more civilized than the Brits had made out, and they welcomed the soldier from the dance, soon known to all as "Robbie", into their home.

Things progressed quite nicely and, in March of 1946, a wedding was held at the little church around the corner. Even though the war in Europe was over, times were still very tough in Holland; basic necessities were scarce, and luxuries were non-existent. Still, family and friends arranged a lovely service, with the groom looking sharp in his uniform and the bride beautiful in a dress put together by her sisters, and wedding slippers salvaged from a bombed-out shoe factory. After the ceremony, the happy couple drove off in their bridal carriage, an Army Jeep.

Dad had volunteered for the Occupation Army so he could remain in Europe longer, but a couple of months after the wedding, he received word that he was going to have to leave his new bride behind because his duties had ended and he was being shipped home.

On May 6, he landed back in Nova Scotia aboard the *Ile de France*. In August the *Queen Mary* arrived at Pier 21 carrying hundreds of war brides from Holland, England, France, Belgium and several other countries. Mom had left all her family behind in a war-torn land to come by herself to a new country to start a new life with someone she had known for a relatively short time under less-than-ideal circumstances.

**Ben Robicheau**

As someone who had spent her whole life in a large city, Mom's first impression of Halifax was that it was a bit small, but that if this was what Canada was like, she could live here. The next morning, they started out for Westport. She was surprised, as they travelled along, that there were no more cities, only small towns and villages and lots of trees. The farms and fields of the Annapolis Valley reminded her a bit of the agricultural area around Nijmegen, but by the time they were starting down Digby Neck she was beginning to wonder if maybe she had made a mistake.

Then the fog set in.

Crossing the first ferry was a bit concerning, but when they drove onto the second ferry at Grand Passage, she thought she had reached the end of the world, not sure if she believed her new husband that there really was an island over there through that fog.

If she thought Halifax was small, Westport in 1946 must have been a real shocker. Many of the women who had come over on the ship with her had similar experiences, some coming from cities like London or Paris to join their new husband on his "farm" or "ranch", only to find themselves living among the blackflies in a primitive log cabin in Northern Ontario, or in a sod hut miles from their nearest neighbour on the Prairies. Some of these women took one look, turned around, and headed back to where they had come from. Most, like my mother, put their trust in the man they had married and decided to make a go of it.

Things must have been difficult at first. For one thing, although they had been married half a year, this was their first chance to really get to know each other. Mom was an ocean away from her family, in an environment quite different from what she was used to; she didn't speak the language, and could understand very little of what people said to her. She had to get used to being a wife, and at the same time, learn to deal with unfamiliar customs and products. On one occasion Dad came home for supper to find Mom sitting in the kitchen crying. She said she had wanted to make a nice meal for him, but as hard as she had tried, she just couldn't beat the lumps out of the tapioca pudding.

Despite the problems with pudding, things must have worked out all right, because within a couple of years a tradition was started at the Robicheau household, one that would become a more-or-less regular event. A baby was born, the first of many as it was to turn out, all born at home except for one.

When my mother was expecting Ruth Ellen, the doctor in Freeport was going to be away at the expected time of birth, so he advised her to go stay with her parents, who, along with most of the family, had arrived from Holland and were living in Saint John. He thought having easy access to a hospital might be a good idea, since it was the middle of winter and an emergency trip to Digby over frozen roads might be too hard on a pregnant woman

**Ben Robicheau**

My grandparents lived at the bottom of a dip between two steep hills, on a dead-end road along the Saint John River. Ruth Ellen announced she was arriving just after midnight in the middle of a freezing rain storm. When the taxi arrived to take my parents to the hospital, it came down the icy hill with no problem, but was unable to get back up.

Meanwhile, Ruth Ellen was getting more insistent, and finally the taxi driver, after several failed attempts to get back up the slippery hill, called another cab and told him to stay on the other side of the hill, he then drove up as far as he could. My parents got out of the cab and, afraid of falling on the ice, made their way over the hill to the other taxi on their hands and knees. My mother says that as she crawled up the hill, stopping every few feet to have a contraction, and sliding her suitcase full of maternity supplies along in front of her, it occurred to her that, all things considered, she might have been better off staying home.

Eventually, Mom's personal experience with birthing babies grew to the extent that she was considered by people on the Island to be a bit of an expert on the subject. She advised mothers-to-be on how to prepare for their new arrival, and even assisted with some of the deliveries. The doctor would call and let her know when he was leaving for someone's house and she would meet him there. There were a few times when Mom and baby both arrived before the doctor did. My mother helped several current residents of the Island into the world.

## Two Ferries Out

A long time ago, in a place far, far away, a young Dutch girl accepted an offer to dance from a soldier. Now married for over seventy-five years, she's mother to nine kids, Oma to thirteen and Great-Oma to several more.

The things that can develop from a simple waltz!

**Ben Robicheau**

*Aunt Frieda, Virginia, Mom and Ruth Ellen in front of our old house*

## 5: This old house

The house that my father brought his new bride to was one that he had inherited while serving overseas, when his grandfather passed away. By the time Dad returned from the War, he was a newly married man and in need of a place to live.

Unfortunately, by this time, the Brier Island house had been sitting empty for a while and had deteriorated somewhat. Like many other houses on the Island, it was built on sloping land, facing towards the harbour with the front supported by a four-foot stone foundation and the back of the house practically sitting on the ground. This design, with the wooden back sills so close to the ground, resulted in them rotting out, causing the kitchen floor to sag and drop about six inches.

Since his new bride would be arriving in a few weeks, Dad got to work fixing the old place up, replacing the sills and levelling the floor. It occurred to him that indoor plumbing might be a nice touch, too, so he converted a pantry off the kitchen into a bathroom. This gave Dad an opportunity to put the metal-working skills he had picked up in the Army to good use by building his own zinc-lined shower stall. This was the house in which I and most of my siblings were born, and where I lived for the first fifteen years of my life.

**Ben Robicheau**

This old house, which was already old when I was born there over seventy years ago, was in many ways a good example of a typical Island home. It wasn't a fancy house; in fact, the only thing about it that could be considered even remotely fancy was the decorative pressed-tin ceiling in the living room. The rest of the house was what you might call plain but practical. It was a square, wooden-shingled structure with eight rooms, four downstairs and four upstairs, equally divided on either side of a central hall and stairway.

Someone looking at our house from the front would see four front-room windows, two on either side of a front door that I can't remember ever being used; everyone went in and out through the porch door at the back of the house. Because of the way the roof sloped down to just above the living room windows, this observer might think that he was looking at a single-story home; but in fact there was a pair of second-story windows at each end of the house, one for each bedroom. Because they were tucked up close under the roof, all of the bedrooms had sloping walls. This made it a bit difficult to stand up in places; but still, they were roomy enough.

My parents room was on the south side of the house, next to the smallest bedroom that was used as a nursery for the latest arrival. Across the hall at the front of the house, my sisters shared a room which gradually grew more and more crowded as their numbers regularly increased.

My own room was on the north end of the house at the back, and from my window I could see across the harbour to Fish Point. There was a streetlight on my side of the house, and at night the light shining through the tree at the bottom of Stanley's Lane threw constantly moving, shadowy designs on my sloping bedroom wall. In the summertime, it sometimes got warm up in those rooms, although that wasn't usually a big problem in Westport; it was when the winter winds blew that you really noticed the lack of insulation and central heating in the old place.

Most of the houses on the island had very little in the way of what we would consider insulation. Some people had discovered during renovations that previous owners had made some attempt at weatherproofing. A fairly common way to cut down on drafts was to cover gaps in the outer wall by plastering the inside of the wall with old newspaper pages, or sometimes with strips of birch bark. Walls were also stuffed with such things as horsehair, balled up newspaper, sawdust, wood chips, or old clothing. We once found that an attempt had been made to insulate a section of wall in our house by stuffing it with dried seaweed.

Every fall, we laboriously installed heavy, wooden-framed storm windows. Still, there was many a winter's night when I could feel the draft all the way across the room, as the wind rattled and whistled in around my bedroom window. On those exceptionally cold nights, Dad would come into my room and spread his old Army greatcoat over my bed for extra warmth.

After reading in bed for a while, I would dread having to get out of the warm nest I had made to reach the little pull-chain to turn off the bare bulb that hung from a cord in the middle of my room. Eventually I got smart and tied a string from the chain to my bedpost, so all I had to do was stick one arm out into the cold to turn off the light.

In the morning, if the wind had been from the North, the inside of my window might be decorated with a swirly frost design; and, more often than not, there would be a little snowdrift on the inside sill, or on the floor below the window. Getting out of a nice warm bed on such a morning could be a challenge; hitting that ice-cold linoleum with my bare feet was not something I looked forward to. Often, I would just leap out of bed, grab my clothes, and rush downstairs to change beside the living room oil stove that struggled in vain to provide heat for the whole house.

Even though our family was steadily growing and we could use the space, for some reason we only occupied half of our main-floor rooms. At some time before we moved in, the house had either been built to be a two-family home, or had been converted to accommodate another resident; whatever the reason, it had two kitchens and two living rooms.

For a few years after they immigrated to Canada, my grandparents and some of my uncles lived in this other side of the house. My grandfather had been a

## Two Ferries Out

baker in Holland, and I can still remember the wonderful smell of his just-out-of-the-oven raisin bread coming from the kitchen across the hall. After he got a job at Eastern Bakery in Saint John and they moved away, the front room became a playroom for us kids and the kitchen became a storage area for various odds and ends.

We probably used that kitchen for storage because our house didn't have a basement that was easily accessible. The house was built on a stone foundation that provided just enough room for a crawl-space. If you really needed to get beneath the house, a small door in the foundation wall allowed limited access.

The only other way to get in under there was by going down into the root cellar. In the front hall beside the stairs was a removable section in the linoleum floor covering. Beneath this was a hatch in the floor, and a short set of steep stairs leading to a small, stone-walled, dirt-floored room.

I didn't mind going down into the root cellar in the early fall right after Dad had returned from his annual trip up to the Annapolis Valley, where he traded fish for produce with the farmers. After he had wrestled the resulting several bags of potatoes, barrel of apples, and all the other various fruits and vegetables that were meant to sustain us through the winter months down the steep, awkward steps, the root cellar was kind of nice. The scent of the apples and potatoes, the bags of onions, the boxes of turnips and squash, all combined to overpower the naturally musty, damp-earth smell and gave me a secure feeling that we were well prepared for the coming winter.

A few months later, it was quite a different story. By spring, the odour down those stairs was a strong blend of rotting fruit and vegetables combined with the musty, claustrophobic, winter-long dampness of earth that had never seen the sun. Reaching into the dark bottom of the apple barrel with great reluctance, I could anticipate the sensation of my fingers breaking through the skin of a decaying Macintosh; the half-deflated bag of potatoes in the corner would have ghostly-looking pale-white tendrils growing through the rancid-smelling, black, rotten potato-juice-stained burlap. The spongy, slimy onions would be competing with the potatoes to see who could grow the longest sprouts, and any squash or pumpkins left would be sitting in a row with their heads slowly caving in. Of course, the turnips, the vegetable that I liked the least, survived the winter in pretty good condition—if you overlooked the places where the mice had nibbled on them.

One spring day, my neighbour Roger and I were sitting out in our front yard with my new Daisy Lever Action BB gun, shooting at cans and bottles lined up on the breastwork across the road. To recock the gun after every shot, you had to swing down and pull back up again a lever under the trigger. Because it was new, the spring that was being reset with this action was very stiff, and Roger had difficulty performing the required action. He tried several different ways of cocking the gun, and found that by putting the barrel over his shoulder pointing backward, he was able to pull down the lever.

The second or third time he did this, he must have accidentally held down the trigger, because as soon as he cocked the gun, it fired. The BB went straight through one of the front window panes and across the living room, where it ricocheted off the wall above the couch and just a few inches from the nose of my father, who was having a little lie-down before going back to work.

By the time he got to the window to confirm what he already suspected was the source of this missile, Roger was well on his way home and all my father saw in the front yard was me, holding my Daisy Lever Action and trying my very best to look as innocent as I actually was.

When I was fifteen, we moved out of this house and a few years later my father sold it to a lady from New York who used it as a summer home. Since then, the old place has been renovated inside and out. It even has a full basement under it now. It looks a lot nicer than it did, somehow straighter, maybe a bit more sophisticated than when it was our family home; but despite the changes I know that, deep down in its wooden bones, it still holds my childhood memories, and that it is still the same old house that I grew up in.

**Ben Robicheau**

## 6: How the Department of Immigration saved my life

As Long and Brier Islanders well know, one of the disadvantages of living in this unique and beautiful, but relatively remote, part of the Province has always been the lack of certain services that people on the mainland take for granted. The one service that's probably the most important to most people is health care.

Years ago, the Islands were one of the first places in the Province to be chosen as a test site for the then-unique position of nurse-practitioner; and although the experiment itself has more or less worked out, and most people are more than happy to have a clinic and health-care provider available, finding a qualified nurse-practitioner who can adapt to the Islands lifestyle and, at the same time, keep the powers-that-be happy, seems to be an elusive and on-going challenge.

Up until sometime in the 1980s, the Islands had their own resident doctor, the result of a government program that seemed designed to attract doctors to Canada, mostly from Great Britain. The reward for agreeing to serve for a certain length of time in some far-flung, under-served corner of the province was a faster and easier trip through the immigration process.

Freeport, Long Island, qualified as one of these remote locations. The aspiring new Canadians would move into the big old doctor's house on the main road near the foot of Crocker's Hill that was a combination family residence, medical clinic and pharmacy, and usually stay for the required minimum number of years before moving on and being replaced by another British newcomer. This revolving-door system of attracting doctors was not exactly an ideal situation, but for the most part it worked.

In fact, in some ways it worked very well. The people who came here were usually well-educated, often were coming from big cities where they had had access and exposure to the latest developments, and generally had spent time working with considerably larger populations, so acquired a much wider experience base than the typical country doctor. This put us in the unique situation of often having a medical service that was in some ways equal or even superior to what was available in many other parts of the province. In fact, I believe that if this system had not been in place, I would not be alive today.

My parents, having succeeded in getting themselves both on the same continent and setting up housekeeping in a fine old house, had taken the next logical step and started a family. They started with me.

My arrival, upstairs in my parents' bedroom, was probably not too out of the ordinary for the times

## Two Ferries Out

and the location. My father had to go to the other island to get the doctor, and I was born while they were both on the ferry on their way back. I was delivered by Dot, the local midwife. No complications; apparently a healthy baby boy.

When I was only a few days old, my parents noticed that I was not able to keep food down. Various well-intentioned people advised the first-time parents not to worry, I probably just needed to get used to eating—or maybe they were feeding me too much —or maybe it was too little—or possibly I was swallowing too much air as I ate. Despite all this helpful advice, things continued to deteriorate, and they became more concerned as I began to get lethargic and lose weight.

Worried, they took me to Digby Hospital, where it was determined that I was most likely suffering from an allergy to mother's milk and putting me on formula would solve the problem. After several days on formula, I still was not doing any better, so it was back to Digby, where the advice now was to try a different formula. This did not help either, and by now I was almost a month old and getting dangerously malnourished, dehydrated and weak.

While all this was going on, a Dr. O'Reilly had arrived in Freeport from Dublin, Ireland, and my father, now feeling desperate and not so confident in the advice he had been getting from Digby, decided to give the new doctor a call.

Dr. O'Reilly listened as my father described my symptoms, then to his shock and confusion, immediately hung up the phone without saying anything. Twenty minutes later he was standing in our kitchen giving me an examination. After seeing my violent reaction to being fed, he told my parents he thought he knew what was wrong; I appeared to be suffering from a condition called pyloric stenosis; but to be absolutely sure, he wanted a second opinion. Fortunately, Dr. O'Reilly's wife was also a doctor, so I was bundled up and taken to Freeport.

While my parents waited at the ferry slip, my grandfather, not generally an emotional man, appeared and asked to see me. He later told my mother that he wanted to say good-bye because he was sure it was the last time he would see me alive.

Once we got to Freeport, Mrs. Dr. O'Reilly examined me, and, without being told what her husband suspected, almost immediately diagnosed the problem as being pyloric stenosis.

Pyloric stenosis is a condition that appears in approximately three out of every one thousand infants. It appears almost exclusively in first-born children, is four times more common in boys than girls, and is almost always fatal if left untreated. The over-development of a certain muscle constricts the bottom of the stomach, shutting off the entrance to the intestines. Since the stomach contents can't exit in the normal manner, it all goes back the way it came, resulting in what is accurately described as "projectile vomiting".

Although the effects of pyloric stenosis were first observed in 1717, it wasn't until 1887 that, through autopsies of infants, doctors discovered the cause and could provide a diagnosis as a medical condition. Although there were earlier attempts to rectify the problem with surgery, it wasn't until 1917 that a Dr. Ramstedt came up with an operation that reliably corrected the condition without killing more patients than it saved. Even today, it is not known exactly what instigates the muscle thickening that causes pyloric stenosis to occur.

With both the Drs. O'Reilly agreeing on the diagnosis, and considering my rapidly deteriorating condition, it was decided that I had to get to the hospital immediately. Dr. O'Reilly instructed my father to make a phone call and ask for the ferry to be held for us in Tiverton.

When he called the telephone exchange and said he needed to get a message to the ferry, the operator, Charlie Young, filling in for his wife Elsie, informed him that that party line was busy and then hung up.

When Dr. O'Reilly heard this, he said, "Call back, and this time make sure they know it's an emergency."

Upon hearing this, Charlie said, "Why the Hell didn't you tell me that the first time? I'll get those old biddies off the line!"

The next thing Dad heard was some women talking and then Charlie telling them in no uncertain terms that he needed the line.

At first, Digby Hospital was not sure what to make of this newcomer with the Irish accent when he showed up in the emergency room with two distraught parents and a deathly-ill baby. The doctors were reluctant to accept his diagnosis of a condition that they appeared to be unfamiliar with, and even more reluctant when he insisted that the only solution was an immediate operation on a weak and sickly month-old infant. No one at Digby Hospital had ever performed this procedure, and although Dr. O'Reilly had seen it performed just before leaving Britain, he was not yet accredited at the Digby Hospital, and therefore could not perform any procedures himself. His only option was to convince someone else to do the surgery.

The Digby doctors suggested keeping me for observation for a few days to see if they could improve my condition. Dr. O'Reilly insisted that I was rapidly approaching the point of no return: without the operation, my condition was not going to improve, and within a very few more hours I would be too weak to survive the procedure. It had to be done immediately.

Finally, Dr. McCleave stepped forward and said he would attempt it, with guidance from Dr. O'Reilly.

Obviously, the operation was a success, or I wouldn't be here to tell you about it. Dr. McCleave and Dr. O'Reilly were happy to tell my parents that I had survived, but they did warn them that due to the severe lack of nourishment I experienced in my first few weeks of life, there would be ongoing health problems: my growth would probably be stunted, I would most likely be sickly all my life, and I could possibly be mentally deficient.

I eventually grew to be 6'2" and never had any unusual trouble with my health along the way, so I'm happy to be able to say that at least two of their three predictions did not come to pass!

As far as I can tell, I was the first baby to be operated on for this condition at Digby General Hospital, most likely the first in all of Digby County, and possibly the first, or at least one of the first, in the Province. A few years later, Dad happened to run into Dr. McCleave on the street and, after asking how I was doing, Dr. McCleave informed him that, since operating on me, he had performed the same procedure on more than a dozen other children.

By the time I was born in 1948, pyloric stenosis had been well documented in medical literature for well over sixty years, and a reliable solution to the condition had been known for nearly thirty years; yet it took a combination of luck, fate, and the Canadian Department of Immigration to bring Dr. O'Reilly from Dublin to Freeport just in the nick of time, and with the experience to identify my problem, as well as the knowledge to fix it. That, and the willingness of Dr. McCleave to take a chance on the word of someone he barely knew, saved not only my life, but also the lives of many other Digby County kids.

**Ben Robicheau**

*A typical Westport punt.*

# 7: Borrowed boats and broken bones

Although Dr. O'Reilly holds a special place in the hearts of my parents (and me!), he was only one of the many doctors who served the Islands over the years. Early on, there were the two Drs. Weir, father and son. Dr. Weir the younger took over the practice from his father. He used to transport his bicycle across the passage in a dory, and would then ride around town doing house calls.

Later on, some of the doctors would use a punt with an outboard motor to visit patients on the other side of the harbour. I think the same boat may well have been passed along from doctor to doctor; it was probably considered a necessary piece of equipment for anyone practising medicine on the Islands. In the island environment, easy access to a boat makes a lot of sense for someone responding to an emergency; no need to wait for the ferry: just zip across the harbour and land your flat-bottomed boat on the beach right in front of your patient's house.

One fine summer's day, this very punt was hauled up on the beach in front of *our* house. The doctor had been summoned because my mother had gone into labour again. Being only ten years old, I wasn't all that interested in what was going on in the upstairs bedroom, so instead headed down to the beach to have a closer look at the doctor's boat. Upon his arrival, the tide had been receding and the boat was soon left high and dry, but things were progressing slowly at home, and by now the tide was on its way back up again.

As the boat started to re-float, I thought it might be a good opportunity for me to take a little spin around the harbour; I was sure the doctor wouldn't mind, as he was going to be occupied for the next little while anyway.

Pushing off from shore, I discovered a slight problem; the doctor had left the motor tilted up and locked in position, and it took me some time to figure out how to release it. Then, when I did, it occurred to me that I didn't actually know how to operate an outboard motor.

After yanking on the starter cord several times with no positive results, I started thinking that maybe this wasn't such a good idea after all. By now, the tide was starting to carry me along the waterfront and away from the shore, heading farther out into the harbour.

While I was trying to figure out what to do next, my grandmother happened to look out the front window and saw my predicament. My mother was having enough trouble with this baby that didn't seem to want to come out, I'm sure it didn't help matters any when my grandmother ran into the room screaming in Dutch that I was being swept out to sea in the doctor's boat.

## Two Ferries Out

For a few minutes there, I would have been inclined to agree with my grandmother's assessment of the situation. The tide was about to carry me out past the end of my father's wharf and all I could see beyond that were the big green rollers going through the passage between Southern Point and Peter's Island: it looked to me like that was where I was headed.

At the last minute, I realized that there was a pair of oars in the boat, and I started frantically rowing back towards shore. With a lot of awkward struggling and splashing, I managed to get back in close enough to my father's wharf to be able to just catch hold of the outermost post.

When I finally managed to pull myself along the posts to safety back at the beach, there was my father waiting for me. My memory about what happened next is a bit fuzzy, but I do recall that I had difficulty sitting down for a while.

My next experience with an Island doctor took place about a year later. It was a sunny Sunday morning, and I and my sisters were on our way to Sunday School. For some reason, Rikki was, in my opinion, dawdling along, making us late, so I saw it as my Christian duty to make sure she got to Church on time. I performed this duty by chasing her along the Front Road in the general direction of the Church.

As we passed by Malcolm McDormand's fish plant, she tried to get away from me by running off onto the wharf, so naturally I ran after her. This wharf had a very narrow walk-way along the side of the building, with only a single high rail on the open side. Just as I entered this walk-way, the smooth leather soles of my Sunday shoes slipped on the weathered planks, and I went under the rail and over the edge of the wharf.

Fortunately, there was a boat tied up at the wharf, and I hit the bow line on the way down, breaking my fall somewhat. Unfortunately, I wasn't able to hang on to the rope, and I continued to the beach. Fortunately, since I couldn't swim, the tide was out. Unfortunately, that meant I hit the rocky beach pretty hard.

By the time I managed to struggle back up to the road, Edgar McDormand was waiting for me in his big, shiny, pink and black DeSoto. He had been on his way to church when he happened to catch a glimpse of someone falling off his father's wharf.

At this time in Island history, it was generally acknowledged that any adult had pretty much total authority over any child, so I braced myself for a scolding and a lecture about the dangers of playing on the wharf. Instead, he just told me to get in the back seat.

When we started up the road, I told him I needed to go the other way; I was on my way to Sunday School. He said he was taking me home. I insisted that I was going to get in trouble if I didn't continue on to Sunday School. Edgar said, "You're not going to Sunday School. Look at your arm."

## Two Ferries Out

I had rested my arm on the door armrest and when I looked at it, I noticed that the section between my wrist and elbow didn't look quite right. It didn't lie flat: it kind of humped up in the middle.

Up until that point, I had felt shaken up, but in no pain. The moment I realized my arm was broken, the pain came flooding in.

After Edgar delivered me to my parents, they gave me a couple of Aspirin, put my arm in a sling and we headed across the ferry to the doctor's office in Freeport, where an X-ray confirmed that I had indeed broken both bones in my left arm.

Dr. McDonald told me that, to re-set the bones, he would have to pull on my broken arm. I wasn't too thrilled at this prospect, but he told me not to worry, he had something that would fix me right up; I wouldn't feel a thing.

What he had was ether. Ether is a liquid that will knock you out if you breathe the fumes. It is administered medically by placing a rubber mask over your mouth and nose; the liquid is then dripped on a piece of gauze placed in a hole in the mask, and you inhale the fumes. Administering ether can be a fine art; too little ether and you're not completely asleep, too much, and you might never wake up again.

When the doctor placed the mask over my face, I felt like I was suffocating, and the strong ether smell made me choke. I fought the mask and tried to pull it away while Dr. McDonald and my father struggled to hold me down. Finally, everything faded to black, and the next thing I knew, I was waking up with a headache and my arm in a cast.

From what seemed a long distance away, I heard my father asking me how I felt. I told him I was okay, but I had had a very vivid dream about yelling at the doctor. Dad laughed and said, "That was no dream". Apparently, I didn't get quite enough ether, because when Dr. McDonald pulled on my arm, I sat straight up and screamed in his face.

About a month later, I was in my mother's kitchen, sitting across from Dr. McDonald who had come to finally take off my cast. As he laid out his cast-removal implements, he explained that some people get nauseated when having casts cut off, and asked my mother to hold a basin ready just in case.

I was offended by this suggestion, I felt this was a bit unnecessary. I had been living with this thing on my arm for weeks now, it was heavy, itchy, smelly, and awkward; I was thrilled to be finally getting rid of it. I couldn't see me having any problem with its removal.

All was fine as he cut away the part that looped around my thumb and over my hand, but as the shears started working their way up the cast, the sensation of the cold metal sliding against the dry skin of my damaged arm, and the crunching sound it made as it cut through the plaster cast, made my stomach turn somersaults.

As it turned out, Dr. McDonald was absolutely right, the basin did indeed come in handy, and I learned something that I would like to pass along to any of you who might have the misfortune to break a bone or two: It's not a good idea to fill up on red licorice just before having your cast removed.

**Ben Robicheau**

*The Little Store.*

## 8: The Little Store

As a child, I found myself in a situation that many kids could only dream of. On the day I was born, my father took ownership of a small general store, so I grew up in the enviable position of having easy access to everything a young boy could possibly want. It was all there: candy, pop, ice cream, chips, and comic books, as much as I wanted, anytime I wanted, all free for the taking. I could just walk in and help myself to whatever I wanted any time the notion struck me.

At least, that was what many of my friends thought. The reality was quite a bit different.

First, there was the health aspect to consider. Sure, personally, my pre-teen self would have been quite happy subsisting on a steady diet of licorice, chocolate milk, and potato chips, but, understandably, my father didn't quite see it my way. For some reason, he thought it might be a good idea to leave a little bit of room for real food in my system, so he tried, with varying levels of success, to limit the amount of "junk" I consumed.

Also, as time went on and the family continued to grow, it just became too darn expensive to allow everyone in the family unrestricted access to the candy counter. All those ten-cent chocolate bars, nickel bags of Scottie's Chips and seven-cent bottles of pop, multiplied by what was eventually to be nine kids, soon added up. Even with what I considered my father's unreasonably strict limitations on my candy consumption, I was constantly being advised by various people that I was eating up my father's profits.

Since Dad worked in his fish business during the day, and therefore was only in the store in the evenings, the bulk of the responsibility as guardian of the goodies fell to his day-time clerk, Gladys Bailey. There were many days where Gladys spent more time arguing with us kids over how many Fudge-Stiks was too many for one person to consume than she did waiting on customers. Gladys was a staunch adversary, and could put up a good argument, but as the family increased, she became badly outnumbered and quite often just gave up in frustration, saying, "Go ahead, take it, I don't care if your father does fire me."

Even when we did lose the odd battle, there were other ways to get what we wanted. In those days of reusable glass bottles, every time you bought a soft drink, you paid a bottle deposit. When you returned the empty bottle to the store, you got the deposit back. A small pop bottle was worth two cents, and a large bottle got you a whole nickel. Any kid in need of some quick money could usually come up with a couple of 'empties' after a little scour around the wharves and fish buildings. Then you could just walk into the store like any other customer and buy whatever you wanted (as long as it didn't cost more than a few cents).

This bottle return system was a kind of forerunner to the recycling system many communities have in place now, except it was run entirely by the bottling companies. They used the bottles over and over. Each store had a wire rack near the pop cooler where you placed your empties. Someone would sort them into wooden crates according to whether they were Coke or Pepsi products, then the delivery guy for each brand would take their bottles back to the plant to be washed out and refilled.

For the most part, this system worked quite well, but it did have a few glitches. Unfortunately, between the time they were bought and the time they were returned to the store, a few bottles were used for purposes for which they were never intended, often coming back with the residue of gasoline, oil or who-knows-what in them. One of the most common uses of an empty pop bottle was as a makeshift ashtray; as a result, occasionally a customer would have the unpleasant experience of discovering a decomposing cigarette butt or some other unidentifiable object floating around in their newly-opened bottle of Evangeline Ginger Ale or Frostie Root Beer.

Digby Dairy used a similar recycle system, cleaning and refilling the empty milk bottles customers returned. I can remember more than one occasion when I grabbed a bottle of nice, cold chocolate milk, popped the cardboard stopper and took a big gulp, only to run gagging and spitting from the store. Apparently, the sanitizing equipment would sometimes fail to remove some of the old sour milk at the bottom of the bottle. Maybe the disposable, one-time-use container is not such a bad idea after all.

Digby Dairy also delivered ice cream. Through most of the fifties, it was in unrefrigerated trucks, so they packed the frozen products in green canvas containers that looked like well-insulated duffle bags. To keep things cold, they packed dry ice in around the frozen items.

Dry ice is frozen carbon dioxide; it is extremely cold and can cause instant freezer burn in anyone that touches it. When it melts, it turns directly from a solid back into a gas. These qualities made it potentially dangerous in the wrong hands, a fact that made it very interesting to us kids. We usually made a point of hanging around when the ice cream man dumped out the leftover ice in front of the store at the end of his delivery. Scattered there on the ground, giving off little waves of vapour, it didn't look all that exciting; but kick it into a puddle of water and all kinds of impressive steaming and hissing took place.

Of course, it didn't take long for someone to figure out how to get even more excitement from this chemical reaction. Kids started bringing empty jars with them on ice cream delivery day: pickle jars seemed to be the jar of choice. Using a stick, you would maneuver some of the dry ice into your jar, screw the lid on tight, then retreat to a safe distance and wait. As the ice turned into gas, our anticipation would build up, along with the pressure in the jar, until it exploded in a satisfying spray of glass and old pickle juice. Surprisingly, given the high possibility of putting an eye out, no one was ever seriously injured in these experiments with exploding ice, except for a few minor cases of frostbite.

Like the milk and the ice cream, almost everything was delivered to the store by truck. Jones Bottling Co. delivered Pepsi products from their plant in Weymouth; the Coke truck came from the Valley as did the Scottie's Potato Chip truck. Willett Fruit delivered fruit and vegetables, Atlantic Wholesalers brought a wide variety of items and Oscar Andrews made a weekly run in his little van to deliver fresh meat from his butcher shop near The Crossroads on Digby Neck.

There were a few of the larger items, like barrels of stove oil, and bags of coal destined for the E. C. Bowers Co., that the coastal freighter "Mohawk" delivered to the warehouse on the end of the breakwater on its regular run back and forth between Yarmouth, Nova Scotia and Saint John, New Brunswick stopping at several communities along the way.

Unlike today, not everything was available all the time; things had a season. In winter, there was not a lot of fresh fruit available, except at Christmas time when Dad would get in a few boxes of oranges and apples for the Christmas stockings. You knew that summer had officially arrived when Popsicles re-appeared in the ice cream freezer.

**Ben Robicheau**

Sometime in August, watermelons would become available. I always thought of watermelon as a really exotic item. There was nothing as luxurious on a hot day, as biting into a cool, crisp slice of watermelon. Unfortunately, watermelon was only available for about three weeks, and I ate so much of it in the first week that I was usually sick of the sight of it by the third week. I think I probably did eat up the profits as far as watermelons were concerned.

Very late in the summer, strawberry season arrived, Dad loves strawberries and he would usually order more than he could sell. As a result we ate a lot of leftover strawberries at our house.

The little store across from the ferry slip was an important place not just to me, but to the whole Island. It was the first business you encountered when driving off the ferry. From its doorway, you could keep an eye on the ferry traffic arriving and leaving, or watch the wharf pile up with wooden traps as the fishermen prepared for lobster season. During the run of a day, most of the people on the island either visited the store or passed by in front of it.

The store was a kind of unofficial community centre that doesn't really exist anymore, a meeting place for the tired and the retired as they sat on the bench by the cast-iron wood stove in a cloud of smoke from hand rolled 'makins', and spent hour after hour discussing the weighty affairs of the world, as well as the latest gossip on the Island. It was a warm refuge from the bitter wind for high-school students waiting to cross on the ferry on a

**Two Ferries Out**

winter morning. It was a place where, even if you didn't have a penny in your pocket, you could still get the necessities of life just by saying, "Put it on the bill."

The building still stands, but it no longer invites the customer or the lounger. The bench is long gone, the windows are boarded over and the door padlocked. It's a storage building for fishing equipment now, but it also stores a lot of my childhood.

In my memory, and in the memory of a diminishing number of others, it will always be "The Little Store".

**Ben Robicheau**

*My first comic book supplier - my father's store.*

## 9: In the comic book corner

I've always been an avid reader; it's something I inherited from my mother. Even in the midst of the hubbub and uproar of raising nine kids, she could always find time to get totally involved in a good book. It was probably her way of getting a bit of a mental break from all those diapers and runny noses!

My mother taught me to read before I started school. When they handed out the Little Red, Blue, and Green Readers on the first day, I polished off all three before the morning was over. Then I found out that this reading material was supposed to last us for the next three months!

In later grades, I often got in trouble for reading ahead. At that time, the whole class was expected to progress through our readers together, taking turns standing beside our desk and reading aloud, the rest of us following along at the excruciating pace of the slowest reader. I would often be caught out when my turn to read aloud came up, because I would usually be several pages ahead of where I was supposed to be, often reading a completely different story. By the time my own children came along, I was glad to see that students were allowed more freedom to advance in subjects at their own pace.

As I got older, I would read anything I could lay my hands on. Since Westport had no library in those days, you had to get your reading material wherever you could find it. The comic strips of the daily *Chronicle-Herald* were a good source of entertainment for a young reader, and the colour comics in the weekend paper were a gold mine, what with the antics of the characters in *Gasoline Alley*, *Major Hoople's Boarding House*, *L'il Abner*, *The Katzenjammer Kids*, *Maggie and Jiggs*, *Mandrake the Magician*, *Terry and the Pirates* and *Dick Tracy* to keep you either amused or in suspense.

Two of my favourite strips were *Andy Capp*, the Cockney layabout who was always fighting with his wife, Flo; and *Smokey Stover*, a fireman who drove a two-wheeled automobile and whose comic strip panels were filled with impossible machines, outlandish but clever puns and ridiculous sight gags. *Smokey Stover* didn't run in the *Chronicle-Herald*. I happened to come across it in a stack of old U.S. newspapers that had been used as padding in a shipping crate.

As I moved along into the stage of reading more serious literature, I began working on longer books like *The Hardy Boys* series, and even some of my sister's, *The Bobbsey Twins*. Then I graduated to books with a little more weight, like *Moby-Dick*, *Ten Years Before the Mast*, *Oliver Twist*, *A Tale of Two Cities*, *Tom Sawyer*, and *Huckleberry Finn*. When I ran out of new material, I would go back to one of my old favourites and read it again; I must have read *Tom Sawyer* half-a-dozen times.

## Two Ferries Out

My mother was a long-time member of the Reader's Digest Classic Book Club, and through this I was exposed to some of history's great literary works. Between the gilt-edged pages of those thick books with the fake leather covers, I discovered wonderful stories like *To Kill a Mockingbird*, *A Tree Grows in Brooklyn*, *The Grapes of Wrath*, *Night of the Hunter*, *Ol' Yeller*, and many others. At the beginning, I wasn't really aware that what I was reading was a condensed version of these stories, and years later I read some of those books again, in their complete and unabridged form; but for many of them, the Reader's Digest version is all I know of what many consider to be some of the great writing of the period.

The years of the '50s and '60s are considered, by those who know about these things, to be the golden age of the comic book, and I spent a lot of my afternoons lost in the coloured-ink panels of *Batman*, *Superman*, *Archie*, *Sgt. Rock*, *The Lone Ranger*, *Lash LaRue*, *Hopalong Cassidy* and even *Donald Duck* and *Little Lulu*.

In addition to the regular ten cent comic book, there was also a twenty-five cent Classic Comics series that tried to slip a little education and culture into the unsuspecting comic reader's repertoire. These thicker, more expensive comics told the story of such historic events as the Civil War, the French Revolution, the sinking of the Titanic, and the building of the railroads across the Western frontier, all in the familiar comic-book format. They also attempted to introduce some of the classics of literature in illustrated form, with severely simplified and revised versions of stories like *The Man in the Iron Mask*, *The Count of Monte Cristo*, *Robinson Crusoe*, *Uncle Tom's Cabin*, and *The Hunchback of Notre Dame*.

Early on, I was lucky to have unlimited access to comic books: my father sold them at his little store near the breakwater. Every month, a new shipment of reading material arrived, and I happily spent countless hours perched on a nail keg or pop bottle crate over in the corner by the rubber boots and oilskins, reading up on the latest adventures of *Chip 'n' Dale* or *Richie Rich*.

Sadly, this idyllic arrangement came to an end when I was about ten years old, when my father decided to get out of the comic and magazine business. I was suddenly forced to go out and find a new supplier to feed my comic book reading habit.

Fortunately, I knew right where to turn: Bowers' Store carried the largest selection of comics on the Island. I had visited Bowers' comic book department many times before, but their comics were displayed in a rotating wire rack that was located right by the store's front counter, convenient if you were just buying, but very awkward for someone wanting to sit or stand there reading comics for any length of time without attracting undue attention or getting in someone's way or running the risk of being stepped on while sitting on the floor. Fortunately, at just about the time I needed a new comic book connection, they rearranged the store and relocated the

## Two Ferries Out

comics to a much quieter, out-of-the-way corner near the end of the candy counter.

My first attempt at taking advantage of this new set-up didn't go well at all. After perusing the comic book selection for a few minutes, I was just about to settle in with the latest edition of *The Incredible Hulk* when one of the old men who usually occupied the bench at the back of the store informed me that if I wasn't going to buy anything, I didn't have any business being there. Apparently, it was okay for these guys to occupy space on the store bench all day, smoking up a storm and arguing a blue streak, but a kid sitting quietly in the corner and reading would be upsetting to the customers!

I didn't give up that easily. I came back later when there was no one on the bench and kept on coming back until they finally decided to just ignore me after they realized I wasn't going to go away. Interestingly, it was only the guys on the bench (some people called them loafers) who ever had a problem with me being there. The only thing I can remember a store employee saying to me was the occasional reminder that I had been there most of the afternoon, it was getting late, and my mother probably had supper ready by now. I spent several years of my life in that corner, but I can't recall any of the clerks, or even Mr. Bowers himself, ever giving me a hard time about sitting there for hours on end, reading all the comic books for free.

The last few years that I was in school, the Bookmobile started to make the Islands a regular part of its route. This library-on-wheels was a great source of reading material, but it only showed up once a month or so, and there was a limit to the number of books you could take out at one time. More often than not, you would finish off your selections in a couple of weeks, then have to wait a couple of more weeks before the Bookmobile returned. It was possible to get around this problem by trading books with a friend, if you could find one who shared your taste in reading material, but the Bookmobile people frowned upon this practice and you ran the risk of getting in trouble with them if your friend wasn't diligent about returning the books you had taken out.

Some time in the mid-seventies, a movement was started to build a library on the island. Through the persistence and perseverance of several dedicated people, it finally became a reality, and today the Westport Library is an important part of the community. Through their own little library, Islanders now have access to the thousands of books and other reference materials in Nova Scotia's provincial library system.

Today I rarely sit in stores for hours at a time and read their books for free, but I still do enjoy a good book, and I am happy to say that both of my kids have inherited a love for literature; a gift from their grandmother that I am more than pleased to pass on.

## 10: Go play outside

Although I was happy to spend countless hours reading, the outdoors was also a huge part of my childhood. Brier Island was yet to be invaded by the electronic baby-sitters. It was still the time before XBox or Wii or portable telephones, a time when you spoke to friends face-to-face instead of on Facebook. The internet, or video games, or computers, or iPods were things that were inconceivable to most of us. I was a teenager before colour TVs became available, and the first VCRs were still a long way off.

In those days, if we kids were looking for adventure, instead of sitting in front of a video screen lost in a virtual world, we just opened the door and walked out into the real world. Parents were more relaxed about their children then; they didn't constantly supervise their kids to make sure they were being entertained or stimulated every second of the day. If you were bored, it was up to you to go find something interesting to do.

On the Islands, we were probably allowed more freedom to roam than most kids. It was not uncommon on a summer's morning to take off for the back shore or Pond Cove and be gone all day. As long as you were home for supper, your parents usually wouldn't give a second thought to your whereabouts. If they did want to find out what you were up to, everyone on the island knew everyone else so there was usually someone who could fill them in on where you were and what you were doing. If a kid was doing something he shouldn't, any adult could order him to "get the devil out of there" and most kids would obey without question; if you didn't, that bit of information always seemed to have a way of beating you home, and you would have to explain yourself to your parents.

But our parents didn't always know everything, and we got pretty good at coming up with projects that would take us out from under the watchful eyes of adults. One of the popular summertime activities was the building of "camps" in the woods. Some of the older boys built quite elaborate ones, complete with bunks and wood stoves, where they would sometimes stay overnight. But most of the camps, although started with grand ambitions and elaborate plans, usually ended up being rather crude lean-tos thrown together with scrap lumber, tree branches and alders. The construction of the camp was usually the most exciting part. Once it was finished, we might visit it a few times before interest would wane and we'd go on to our next project.

In retrospect, it's probably a good thing that our parents were not aware of everything we got up to. Some of our projects and pastimes bordered on questionable as far as safety went, and a few of them crossed right over into being downright dangerous. One summer's day, a group of us were playing "Cowboys and Indians" on the back shore. We had made bows out of alders and arrows out of long straight reeds, and the past several days had been spent in chasing each other all over Harris's Bluff, arguing over who was shot and who wasn't. When a couple of the 'Indians' started shooting pointed arrows made from alders, and one of the Cowboys showed up with a loaded .22 rifle and proceeded to ricochet bullets off a rock some of us were hiding behind, the more reasonable among us decided things were getting a bit out of hand, and that was the end of that game.

Swimming is a common summer activity for many kids, but not so much for us Islanders. Most of the fishermen on the island did not know how to swim, the thinking being, why bother? If you fell overboard in the Atlantic, you most likely would be too far from land to swim to safety anyway, even if you managed to somehow survive the always-frigid waters. They passed this attitude on to their children, and as a result, a lot of island kids of my generation did not bother to learn how to swim, I myself only learned in my early teens while visiting my grandparents, who lived on the Saint John River.

Still, there were a few who dared to brave the chilly waves, and they would take advantage of those rare days each summer when it warmed up enough to tempt some of the hardier souls into the cold water that is all we have available to us. Pond Cove was a popular spot on those days when the sun would warm up the beach sand enough to give the false impression that the water might actually be bearable.

**Ben Robicheau**

There were a few brave souls who would take the plunge, but the waves rolling into the cove were coming straight out of the cold Atlantic and it would only be minutes before blue lips, uncontrollable shivering and the real possibility of hypothermia became a concern. Occasionally someone would try swimming on the pond side of Pond Cove where the water was warmer, but this still water was also stagnant, and getting out to where it was deep enough for swimming required wading up to your knees through stinking black mud.

Instead of going all the way to Pond Cove, some kids would swim off the wharves right in town. The usual procedure here was to jump off the wharf into the water, swim quickly to shore before your extremities went numb, warm up a bit, and repeat. One summer when I was about nineteen, some kids were jumping off Melbourne McDormand's wharf next to the ferry slip. It had been a long time since I had had a dip in the harbour, it looked like they were having fun, and the water temperature near the beach felt bearable, so I decided to give it a try.

It was about a ten-foot drop from the wharf to the water surface, so when I jumped, I went in deep. The water that far down was so cold, that the shock gave me an instant headache and took the breath right out of me, it felt like I didn't have enough left in my lungs to get back to air. When I finally did struggle to the surface, I headed straight to shore, and that was the last time I went swimming in Westport.

## Two Ferries Out

Another popular pastime on the Island was rowing. The small, flat-bottomed boats that fishermen used to get themselves out to where their fishing boats were moored in the harbour were referred to as 'punts'. These were often home-made craft, built by the fisherman himself, and some took a lot of pride in their work and were quite protective of them. But most didn't mind if you borrowed their punt as long as you returned it in good condition and tied it up properly, so we often spent many hours rowing back and forth along the waterfront. Every once in a while, someone would overestimate their rowing abilities and a rescue mission would have to be mounted to retrieve some frantic kid from the tide that was about to carry him and his borrowed craft out through the passage. To avoid this kind of disaster, the smaller kids would leave the punt tied by its bow or stern line and just row back and forth the length of the rope: enjoying the fun of rowing without the risk of being swept out to sea.

As small children, Natalie, Wendy and Angela Gower would enjoy little rowing excursions in Duffy Frost's punt, until one fateful evening when they realized, too late, that the light was fading and they weren't sure that they could get back to the wharf before total darkness fell. The girls were beginning to panic, imagining being lost on the ocean at night, when Angela saved the day by hiking her dress up around her waist, jumping over the side and pulling the punt and her terrified sisters in to shore. Angela was a hero to her sisters, who believed she had saved their lives; a feeling that didn't diminish even after they later remembered that the bow line had been tied to the wharf the whole time, and they had never been more than a few feet from shore.

Of course, being surrounded by water, fishing was a natural pastime. We would fish off the wharves for harbour pollock in the summer and "frost fish" in the winter. I'm not sure what the difference was between the two; they looked the same to me. I think the term "frost fish" may describe more the act of fishing than the fish. Any kid who has sat on the end of a wharf in winter trying to jig a fish knows firsthand about frost.

## Two Ferries Out

Most of the fish we caught were too small to be of much use anyway. Generally we cut them up for bait to catch more fish, fed them to the cat, or maybe used them for lobster bait if you had a lot of them. Once in a great while, you might catch a fish big enough to actually take home for supper.

One Saturday when I was about twelve years old, my friend and neighbour David Nickerson and I were fishing off the ramp at my father's fishplant. David managed to get his hook caught in the side of the wharf, so I leaned over the edge and reached way down to unsnag it. I reached just a little too far, and the next thing I knew, I went headfirst over the side of the wharf and sank rapidly down through twenty feet of water.

As the hip-boots I was wearing filled with water, they dragged me down feet-first, so I found myself standing upright on the harbour floor. This was well before I learned how to swim, and even if I had had that skill, it would have been an impossibility with these boots on. The idea of kicking off my boots didn't enter my mind for a second: they were brand-new and my father had warned me not to ruin them by getting water in them. I figured I was in enough trouble already for getting them wet. There was no way I was going to tell him that I had deliberately left them on the bottom of the harbour!

Standing on the ocean floor, contemplating the unusual predicament I now found myself in, I happened to notice a pole nearby. I pulled myself up it, hand-over-hand. When I broke the surface, there was David, waiting to pull me to safety; but my wet clothes and water-filled boots dragging me back to the ocean's depths proved to be too much.

Just before I was pulled under again, I told David, "Meet me on the beach.." Since getting back up onto the wharf had proven too difficult, I had come up with a much simpler plan: I'd just walk to shore.

Using the wharf's support posts as a guide, I trudged along the harbour bottom until I was on the point of running out of air, then I'd shinny up a post until I broke the surface, take a breath, then drop back down to continue my underwater walk. When I finally reached the beach and emerged, streaming water like some creature from the depths, David was waiting with tears streaming down his face. I'd never seen him cry before, and was touched that he was so emotional about my situation.

"I'm okay," I told him. "You don't need to be upset. I didn't drown."

"I wasn't worried you might drown," David replied. "I was worried I'd get blamed for it."

## 11: Breastwork blues

When they told us Island kids to go play outside, one of the places we had available to us was the beach. The beach was a great play area, and for many of us it was right there in front of our house. But to get to it, we had to climb down over the breastwork.

Varying in height from a couple of feet to ten feet or so, the breastwork was a protective wooden cribwork wall, constructed of heavy timbers, that ran along the waterfront. It presented a solid face to the sometimes-violent sea, a barricade to the elements, a defence against the eroding force of the ocean.

For a small child, the breastwork could be an imposing structure. It looked a scary long way down to the beach when you peered over the edge, there was always the possibility of falling off of it onto the rocks below, and it was usually difficult to climb up and down; but not impossible. The timbers were stepped back slightly as they were stacked horizontally on top of each other, so every ten inches there was a little ledge which provided just the slightest bit of a toe-hold. As soon as we were able to master the trick of scaling the wall, going up and down to the beach became second nature.

It's not surprising that the beach was a popular place to play. The breastwork back then more or less took the place of a Jungle Gym today. You could walk along it, one foot in front of the other as on a balance beam, climb up and down it like monkey bars, jump off it onto the beach if the tide was down, or, if you dared to brave the cold, right into the water when the tide was up.

Also, in those days before community garbage collection and before we all became more environmentally conscious, "throw it off the breastwork" was a commonly-heard phrase from someone wanting to dispose of something, so for us kids, the beach was an unending source of interesting items. Some of us went about our daily travels along the beach, as much as we did along the road, in the hope that we might find something good before it got washed out to sea.

My sisters often looked for abandoned treasures among the empty cans and old newspapers. They would spend hours playing house on the beach, setting the table on top of the breastwork with shells and tin cans and decorating the breastwork "walls" with bits of beach glass and pretty rocks and various bits of broken household cast-offs.

The wooden timbers also provided a form of entertainment for the older boys, who chiselled their initials and other designs into them. And I know of at least one teenage artist who skilfully carved the shape of an anchor into the top of the wall, then melted some scrap lead in a fire on the beach and used the breastwork to mould little lead anchors.

The breastwork was fun in other ways, too I remember one time when we played what, in retrospect, was a bit of a mean trick on Madeline Lent! Ed Pugh had been cutting the long grass along the side of the road and all this cut grass had been gathered up and dumped in one spot over the breastwork onto the beach. My neighbour Roger and I had been jumping off into this mound when we noticed Madeline walking up the road. We knew that she couldn't see the hay pile from the road, so when she got close, we stood on the breastwork, pretended to lose our balance, screamed and fell over. Madeline, being the kind-hearted person she was, rushed over to the breastwork, only to see us laughing on a pile of hay a couple of feet below. We thought it was hilarious at the time!

In addition to its comedic possibilities, the breastwork had other attractions. It conveniently blocked the view of the upper few feet of beach from anyone on the road side of it, so it was possible to sit on the beach right in front of your own house and nobody could see what you were doing. Where the breastwork went under a building, it provided an even more secure hiding place. I once found an open pack of cigarettes and a book of matches placed on a beam under a wharf; obviously someone had been doing some secret smoking under cover of the breastwork.

The top of the breastwork was more or less level with the road that ran parallel to it, and this sometimes was a problem when cars and trucks would occasionally end up on the wrong side of it. If you did find yourself on the beach somehow, whether on purpose or otherwise, the wooden wall could be an obstacle to getting back onto the road.

Luckily, the breastwork was not completely continuous. There were a few gaps in the breastwork that provided places for fishermen to haul up their boats or pull something down onto the beach. Also, just about every wharf had a small ramp beside it, going from the beach to the top of the breastwork, so a punt could be hauled up to safety in case of bad weather.

The breastwork wasn't an obstacle only for people. We had a pet seagull named Charles DeGull who, since he was raised by humans, didn't know how to fly and was also afraid of water!

My sister Virginia decided to take Charlie under her wing, so to speak, and taught him to fly by coasting him off a small hill in our front yard, and to swim by floating him out in the water on a board, and then yanking it out from under him. After indignantly swimming back to shore a few times, he realized he liked the water and would walk across the road to the breastwork, jump off and glide down to the beach. After enjoying his swim, he would walk back up the beach to the bottom of the breastwork and yell until someone came and lifted him up to the road. Eventually he figured out that he could fly up as well as down!

**Two Ferries Out**

*Ruth Ellen with Charles DeGull*

Living close to the shore has a lot of benefits. With just a glance out the living room window, you can keep track of ferry crossings, tell if the tide is coming in or going out, and see what is going on in the harbour. Practically every house in the village of Westport has some view of the water, most have waterfront property and many are just a literal stone's throw from the beach.

**Ben Robicheau**

Unfortunately, living across the road from the breastwork also comes with the occasional downside. This was made devastatingly clear to me one day when I was about five years old.

It was a rare, fog-free summer's day in Westport and my mother was out in the yard hanging some of the endless laundry on the line. My friend Wallace and I were in the driveway beside our house, fooling around in my father's nearly new '54 Chev pickup truck. Wallace was riding shotgun while I was behind the wheel, turning knobs and pushing on the pedals. At some point, I must have pulled the gearshift, because the truck suddenly started to move.

I remember kicking at what I assumed was the brake pedal, but the truck only continued to pick up speed. I yanked desperately on the emergency brake lever to no discernible effect. At this point, my mother was running screaming from the clothesline, the truck was rolling even faster, and I was out of ideas on how to stop it.

With a look of fear, Wallace asked, "What are we going to do?"

I replied, "I don't know about you, but I'm jumpin'."

I went out my door and he went out his.

I picked myself up, to see my two-year-old sister Rikki lying flat on her back in the middle of the driveway, and just in time to watch the truck disappear over the breastwork.

It didn't occur to me at the time, but the reason my mother was screaming was that, when the truck

## Two Ferries Out

began to move, Rikki was sitting on the ground directly behind it. As the truck started to roll backwards down the hill, the spare tire attached to the bottom of the truck bed bumped Rikki in the forehead and slowly pushed her flat on the ground, allowing the truck to safely pass over her.

I was unaware of all this. I was fixated on what was happening to that truck.

Our driveway ran downhill to the Front Road, immediately on the other side of the road was the breastwork and an eight-foot drop to the beach. The tide happened to be all the way up, so when the truck went over the edge, it landed in about six feet of water, and, as Wallace and I watched in disbelief, began to slowly drift away.

Apparently, the air in the tires, the wooden floor of the truck bed, and air trapped under the cab roof provided just enough buoyancy to keep it barely afloat, with just a few inches showing above water. As I looked on, the ebb tide slowly carried my father's new truck out into the harbour.

Luckily, a fisherman unloading his catch nearby happened to notice the oceangoing truck and, before it got too far away, was able to hook his anchor under the bumper and tow it back to shore.

Word travels fast in any little community, and Westport is no exception. By the time the truck was delivered back to the beach, the whole island had arrived to witness our little accident first-hand. I remember standing on the breastwork with everyone else, scared, and crying my eyes out, but at the same time, noticing that, if I leaned out a little, I could see, snaking away into the distance, all the people lined up on the breastwork. I think this was probably the first time I had seen most of the island population in one spot and I must admit that I was just a little bit impressed that I had had a hand in bringing them all together and arranging them so neatly in a line.

As the tide receded, the truck grounded out on the beach and a group of men went to work on it. They removed the gas tank and seat, took the engine apart, and lined up various bits and pieces on the, by now, nearly empty breastwork. Then they towed the partly-disassembled truck to a fresh-water pond where they attempted to flush out the salt. By the time night fell, it was all back together and running again.

Not surprisingly, the truck was never quite the same after that. The window cranks seized up, making the windows inoperable; none of the dashboard gauges worked, so you never knew how much gas you had or how fast you were going; and the bodywork suffered badly from premature and extensive rusting. One day, a couple of years after the aforementioned incident, Dad was on his way to Digby when he hit a bump and the cab of the truck suddenly dropped down around his ears. The cab supports had rusted completely away.

He managed to make it to McDonald Motors, where he traded his three-year-old truck in on a new one. They gave him fifty dollars on the trade.

## Two Ferries Out

This was not the first of my father's vehicles to end up on the beach. A few years previous to this incident, he owned a car with which he ran an informal taxi service. One day he was hired on short notice to take some passengers to Digby. Before picking up his fares, he hurried home to freshen up a bit. He straightened up from washing in the kitchen sink just in time to see his car roll past the window and down the driveway. Running outside, he witnessed a scene nearly identical to the one I caused a few years later. Only this time the tide was down and the car, after rolling over the breastwork and luckily managing to stay on its wheels, bounced down the beach and stopped at the water's edge.

Dad was relieved to find his car relatively undamaged, but his next problem was how to get it off the beach. The tide was rising and the breastwork was far too steep to get the car back up over it. There was a break in the breastwork where some of the fishermen pulled up their boats for the winter, but it was on the other side of the fishplant.

Normally this would have been a problem, as the building stretched from the breastwork to beyond the low-water mark, effectively barring the way for any vehicles that happened to be driving along the beach. But, as luck would have it, just the day before, a neighbour had been in the same all-to-familiar situation; car on beach, tide rising, fishplant in the way. He had resolved his dilemma by removing a few of the supporting posts from under the wharf, allowing him to drive through to the other side, and back up onto the road. The posts hadn't been replaced yet, so Dad was able to take advantage of the situation and return his car to the correct side of the breastwork.

Everything seemed to have worked out. He rescued the car in a matter of minutes and picked up the passengers on time, and they were able to catch the ferry on schedule. It was only later, as they made their way up Digby Neck, that it became apparent that the unexpected trip to the seaside may have caused a problem. The farther they went, the slower the car would go until finally, going up Sandy Cove Hill, it came to a complete stop.

Looking the car over for damage, Dad noticed that the tailpipe had been jammed up against the bumper and was now pinched almost completely shut. Carbon build-up from the restricted exhaust had slowly strangled the engine until it lost all power.

To rectify the problem, he borrowed a hacksaw and cut the end off the pipe. When he started the engine, it blew out a huge cloud of black smoke, and by the time they got to Digby, the car was running normally again.

Although we may possibly hold the record, we weren't the only people to have vehicles end up on the beach. As mentioned above, at least one of our neighbours had a similar experience. And a regular visitor to the Island, Bill Bent the travelling meat man, had a near-beach experience one day when he came out of a customer's house to find his truckload of meaty delicacies teetering precariously on the edge of the breastwork. One rear wheel was hanging in mid-air ten feet above the beach, and the truck had stopped just inches from going completely over the edge.

A group of workers from a nearby fishplant rushed to the rescue with a load of wooden pallets, which they stacked up on the beach to support the dangling wheel until the truck could be pulled back onto the road. I don't know if Bill Bent rewarded his saviours, but he probably should have. After all, these guys had literally "saved his bacon"!

Every time I visit Westport now, I am nostalgic for the way it used to be before the Groundhog Day storm of 1976 forever rearranged the waterfront. One of the major changes was the loss of nearly all of the old wooden breastwork that stretched pretty well the whole length of the village, giving it a solid and unified look.

There are still a few sparse remnants of the old breastwork left, but as it continues to deteriorate, the last remaining fragments are being replaced with more of the big armour-stone boulders. At the time, dumping rock was a fast and efficient way to repair the damage of the storm, but it sure doesn't have the look or the history of the old wooden breastwork.

**Ben Robicheau**

*The Bank of Nova Scotia – Open one afternoon a week.*

## 12: A spring bike ride

For a young boy on Brier Island, being allowed to explore the beach, the woods, the harbour waters, the fields and hills—in fact, just about every aspect of our surroundings—gave us a great feeling of freedom. As we got a bit older, the trusty (and because of the salt air, often rusty) bicycle provided an additional feeling of freedom and adventure.

That's what I'm up to today, it's early Spring, 1959, I'm ten years old, and today looks like it could turn out to be a beautiful day. The sun is skittering across the ripples on the harbour, and Westport's gravel roads have dried up enough for me to finally take my Christmas present out for a spin.

I pause my new CCM Supercycle at the end of the driveway to consider my limited travel options in the village of Westport. There are only two main roads in town: most people live on either the Front Road, which follows the waterfront, or the Back Road, which parallels the Front Road a bit further inland. Directions to any location in Westport usually include which of these two roads your destination is on, and whether it is 'up the road' or 'down the road'.

Up the road, and down the road, can be extremely flexible and vague descriptions to the uninitiated. Even some Islanders are not entirely clear on the concept. I've always operated on the understanding that, if you are anywhere in the village of Westport and facing the harbour, everything to your right is 'down the road' and everything to your left is 'up the road' from your present location. If your location changes, then what is up or down the road changes, too.

I glance up the road to my left, toward that more elevated section of the island known as the High Knoll, and notice that the boats usually anchored in that part of the harbour are gone from their moorings. Ace and Wick, two of the fishermen who live up that way, must be out hauling traps, taking advantage of the nice weather in these last few days of lobster season. In fact, as I look down the road in the other direction, I see that nearly all of the three dozen or so boats usually in the harbour are gone from their moorings.

Pushing off, I turn out of the driveway and head down the road. I quickly see that even though the muddy gravel is finally starting to dry up, the road is far from smooth. There's still a bit of frost in the ground, so I guess it's a little too early yet for Brad Delaney, the roadmaster, to be out with his ancient road grader, performing the spring ritual of scraping down the bumps and filling in the dips. I proceed on my way, carefully steering between the ridges, ruts and not-quite-dried-up mud puddles.

As I make my cautious way towards the main part of the village, I pass by the familiar buildings that make up my father's fish plant. Dad is partial to the colour blue and his buildings are covered with blue

## Two Ferries Out

asphalt shingles on the sides and green asphalt shingles on the roof. On my right, on the in-land side of the road, sits the two-story building where salt fish are dried and packed in wooden boxes of one hundred pounds each, in preparation for their long trip to the West Indies.

Across the road, built out over the water, is the long, low shed where the fresh fish are gutted and split, then "pickled" in salt brine for several weeks before going across the road to the drier. Protruding from the far end of this building, sloping down into the harbour water, is the narrow ramp where boats unload their catch. As I pass by, I catch a whiff of the woody, fishy scent coming from the smokehouse attached to the corner of the building nearest the road: smoked fish, called Finnan Haddie, in the making.

On the same side of the road, at the bottom of Ed Pugh's lane, is a building that looks like in years past it might have been a store or some sort of business. In the time I've known it, it has been put to a variety of uses, including storage for fishing gear and as a garage for auto repairs. As I pass by the open big double garage doors that now take up most of the front wall, I can see the 'pit' that was cut into the floor so the mechanic could stand on the beach and work underneath the car. This pit could only be used at certain times, because it was flooded on the high tides. The rest of the interior is presently full of large wooden hogshead barrels, used to pickle fish.

I roll along past Herald Thompson's, Ray McDormand's and Charlie Boy's shops with their stacks of wooden lobster traps, neat piles of flat beach stones to use as trap ballast, and mounds of buoys painted in each fisherman's distinctive colours, all my concentration dedicated to trying to stay out of the ruts and avoid the muddy soft spots in the road.

As I pass the stone wall in front of Edna-Fred's house I suddenly hear the aggressive yapping of a dog. Knowing what this signifies, I throw caution to the wind and recklessly splash through mud puddles and over ruts in a desperate attempt to avoid being caught by Mrs. Bowers' little black Scottie dog.

Just when I think I've managed to avoid him this time, I feel the dreaded clamp of his teeth onto my pant cuff, and all of a sudden I'm fighting to keep my balance as I zig-zag across the road. Trying to avoid falling in the half-thawed mud or running into the rocks along the breastwork, I fend off my growling attacker with my right leg, while trying to pedal faster with my left leg. I'm starting to think Blackie is going to win this one, when the sun porch door opens, and to my great relief, I hear Mrs. Bowers order her dog back into the yard.

Having just survived one of the terrors of travelling the Front Road, I am now confronted with another. The old liver factory is an imposing, two-story building where the father-and-son team of Gerald and Albert Baily collect fish livers from the fish plants on the island and cook them in a big vat. They put the resulting liquid into forty-five-gallon drums and ship it off to be made into fish oil products. This building is a scary place to some kids, not only because of the strong cod liver oil smell that comes from it when the vat is in operation, but also because of what takes place on the second floor.

Above the big, sliding ground-level doors are a set of smaller, upper-floor double doors. When these doors are open, passersby can usually see Gerald and/or Albert sitting on an old couch looking out at the road. This is not the scary part; the scary part is that sometimes when you pass by there is another person sitting there, a person you don't recognize. Some kids say that this mysterious figure is a ghost, some say it's a dummy that Albert and Gerald made and some say it is just someone with a mask on.

Whatever it is, usually the apparition just sits there staring out at you, but several kids swear that they have seen him get up and come to the door, demanding to know where they are going, or why they aren't in school. As a result, many kids detour along the Back Road to avoid this strange character.

I am relieved to see that this time the doors are closed; nevertheless, I speed up and hurry past the ominous, red-shingled building with a prickly feeling on the back of my neck and an eerie sense that someone is watching me from that second floor.

After passing by Lou Bailey's well-kept wharf and shed, I come up to one of the oldest structures in Westport. On my left is a one-story building with several tall windows in the front, some of which have been replaced with a set of double doors. Before the big red schoolhouse was built on the Back Road, this two-room building was the Island's school: now Vic Strickland has converted it to a garage for his car. Vic is a loyal Studebaker man. Every few years he gets a brand-new car, and as I pass by, I can see his latest, a green Studebaker Champion, through the small, wavy panes of the old school windows.

Across from Vic's garage stands what I have always imagined to be the sturdiest house in Westport. Russell Swift has the only brick house on the island; in fact, I think it may possibly be the only brick house on Digby Neck. Russell is also the owner of the most feared cat on the island; Toby is a grumpy, twenty pound, long-haired, black and white tomcat that doesn't seem to be afraid of anyone or anything, and has a habit of beating up the neighbourhood dogs.

I pass a few more fish sheds and an old, green double-ender fishing boat that's been retired and left sitting on the side of the road, where it's been rotting away for the past several years. After passing Edgar McDormand's TV repair shop, and then the little green building next to the ferry wharf that houses the post office, I pull up in front of my father's store.

I chat with Gladys, who has been the day-time clerk for as long as I can remember, while fortifying myself with a bottle of Digby Dairy chocolate milk and a bag of Scottie's Chips. Now I'm ready to continue my ride.

As I continue along, I hit a smooth patch of gravel and risk taking my eyes off the road to glance out

## Two Ferries Out

over the harbour. Out near the moorings are a couple of boats unloading their catch at the lobster cars, the floating wooden cages that keep the lobsters immersed in water and alive until they are ready to be shipped to market. Further out, in the mouth of the passage, midway between Long and Brier Islands, the sun is reflecting off the white-painted lighthouse and lightkeeper's house on Peter's Island.

Continuing along, I pass the bank building, open one afternoon a week, then Daniel Kenney's big fish-plant. Next, I make a brief stop to look through the open doorway of Gerald Strickland's machine shop. He's always working on something interesting, and the noisy, complicated, overhead shaft-drive system, with its pulleys and cams and wide, looping leather and canvas belts that power his various saws, lathes and drill presses, is always a source of fascination for me.

The next building along is a large, slightly-ornate structure that used to be Central House, the only hotel on the island. Back in the days when you travelled to Digby by stagecoach, it would leave from here. Today, this is the Co-Op store; enter through the double front doors and you see before you the wide staircase to the rooms on the second floor, now used for storage. The ground floor is taken up by the store: to your left is the lobby where guests once checked in, now the counter where customers check out with their groceries.

As I continue my ride past the string of wharves between the Co-op and Bowers' store at the bottom of the New Lane, I notice that some of the big cast-iron cauldrons that usually sit upside-down on the side of the road in front of nearly every fish shop are turned upright and ready for use again. Soon, fires will be burning under these pots and they will be filled with melted tar, through which men draw new hemp rope and fishing lines. The tar helps prevent deterioration of the hemp by protecting it from rot, and also aids in repelling any sea creatures that might be attracted to the organic material.

As I approach the New Lane, I notice a thick cloud of smoke pouring out of one of the buildings next to Bowers' store: they're running the forge today. In this building, they melt down scrap lead and pour it into moulds to make large fishing weights. Used to keep the fishing lines down in the strong currents around the island, these weights, called 'leads', can weigh up to several pounds each.

Even though all the doors and windows are open, the smoke is so thick I can barely see across the room. Nevertheless, I go in to see if they'll let me turn the crank that blows air through the coal and heats up the fire in the forge. After half an hour of continuous cranking while breathing coal smoke and lead fumes, my arm is getting sore, my eyes are running, and I'm having trouble breathing, so I decide that's enough fun for now, and call it quits.

Outside in the fresh air once again, I notice that it has clouded over and is starting to look like rain, so I decide I'd better head for home. As I turn from the New Lane onto the Back Road, a few scattered raindrops fall. Standing up on my pedals, I race for home, flying past the Oddfellows Hall, Gerald Strickland's movie hall, the school house and the Baptist Church Parsonage, all in a row.

Half-way home, I slow for a truck coming down from the field where they once dried fish on wooden flakes in the sun, then I go all out again, and just make it home before the rain really starts to come down. What started out as a nice sunny day is now a downpour, and might well turn into snow before nightfall.

Just another typical Spring day on Brier Island.

**Ben Robicheau**

*Sliding on Stanley's Lane.*

## 13: Going downhill

As the seasons changed and the unpaved streets of Westport developed into muddy winter roads with icy ruts, bottomless potholes, and half-frozen puddles, we put away our bicycles in exchange for another form of transportation more suited to those winter conditions. Before the advent of motorized sleds like Ski-Doos and Arctic Cats, the biggest, fastest winter vehicle in Westport was the bobsled.

This was a home-built contraption with four steel runners. The two in the back were fixed, and the two in the front could swivel from side to side, providing a modest amount of not-always-reliable steering. The main body of the sled consisted of a board which connected the front and back sets of runners, and was long enough to hold four or five kids sitting in a row. The person at the front was the "steerer", who provided what control he could by pushing on a steering bar with his feet. The person at the back was the "pusher"—as indicated by the name, the pusher would start the sled off by running behind and pushing for three or four steps before making a wild leap and with luck, landing on the last few inches of board not already occupied. A bobsled was built to run on ice, and on a steep hill could attain exciting speeds.

**Ben Robicheau**

There was really only one bobsled run in Westport, and that was on the New Lane, the street that runs straight downhill past the church, ending at the breastwork. This became the go-to bobsled run, due in large part to the efforts of one young man. Edward was a funny guy, always ready with a joke, always trying to make people laugh. Because of this, he was saddled with the unfortunate yet apt nickname of "Clarabell", after a kid's-show clown character.

Clarabell lived with his parents in the last house at the top of the New Lane, just across from the church. I'm not sure how his fascination with bobsleds started, but I imagine he must have looked out his window one winter's day and realized that, with a little help, the hill could provide hours of entertainment.

Every winter, as soon as it got cold enough, he would be out there after supper, occasionally with the help of others, scooping water from the ditch onto the road. Sometimes it would take several nights of diligent watering to produce a suitable layer of ice. They would ice only one side of the road, leaving the other side for cars to travel up and down. Drivers were usually quite accommodating, and would carefully share the road with the sliders and each other. Even the roadmaster, Brad Delaney, would try to avoid spreading sand on the icy side of the lane.

With the moderate and fluctuating weather we often experienced in Westport, the ice-maker's work would sometimes come to naught. Just as a good bed of ice was building up, the temperature might rise by ten degrees overnight, all that effort resulting in nothing but bare ground the next morning.

But on those occasions when the thermometer stayed below freezing for several days in a row, every kid on the island would flock to the New Lane to take advantage of Clarabell's labours. The ice run stretched from the church down past the Back Road, where the hill started to level out. At this point, the prepared ice would end, and you would come to a grinding halt before reaching the usually-busy-by-Westport-standards Front Road.

Occasionally, after a freezing rain or maybe over-enthusiastic watering by the ice makers, you might continue straight on, or, if you reacted quick enough, you could veer off to the right, off the lane and past the Vestry steps, continuing down a short trail that would bring you out near the Irishtown bridge. If you decided to go straight, you had to make a sharp left or right turn where the New Lane ended at the Front Road or, if you had enough confidence in your driving skills, you might continue across the road, make a slight jog to the right, and run off onto Bowers' wharf. This last manoeuvre required an experienced and skilful pilot, there were at least a couple of instances where the unfortunate slider was unable to make the turn, and ended up continuing straight ahead, over the breastwork and onto the beach.

Most of the sliding, like the ice-making, took place after dark, it was colder then, and the ice was a bit harder. There were three or four bobsleds on the island, and kids would also show up with toboggans, one-man sleds, flying saucers, Crazy Carpets, just about anything that would slide. This made for quite a mix of ages and equipment, all going up and down at random, with the big bobsleds periodically thundering down the hill, scattering everyone in their way.

All the while, cars would be passing by, just inches from the barely-under-control sliders. Surprisingly, I don't recall any injuries, although there must have been a few, and close shaves were just laughed off as another part of the fun.

Although the bobsled was the undisputed king of the New Lane, there was one other sliding device that I believe was its equal for excitement and danger, and it wasn't even a real sled.

One summer's day, the Coca-Cola people showed up at my father's store and attached two round red and white signs to opposite ends of the building. A couple of years later, Dad took them down to repaint the store. He was a little slow about putting them back up, and that winter it occurred to us kids that these large, round, metal discs might make good sleds. It took only one run for us to know that those signs would never be going back up on the wall.

Because they were shaped like the plastic "Flying Saucer" sleds that were available at the time, we called the signs by the same name, but in many ways, they were much superior to the store-bought version. Made of heavy gauge steel and about four feet across, they could hold several kids at a time. Because of their size and shape, they would slide well on anything from heavy frost to deep snow, and the lighter the load, the faster they would go.

There was no steering, so you usually went down the hill without knowing exactly where you were going to end up, all the while rotating wildly; this of course, only added to the excitement. Since the inside of this shallow bowl was smooth, painted metal, there was no traction, and nothing to hang on to for the riders, who would slide around and fly up in the air with every bump.

The lip of the saucer was a sharp, unprotected edge, and every once in a while an unfortunate rider would come down hard on this edge. Many of us ended an evening of sliding with crescent-shaped marks on various parts of their bodies.

One day, a group of us were sliding in Shelly Bailey's steep front yard, ending our run at an old picket fence just before the Front Road, when a young lady happened along. Although she was at an age where makeup and hairdos were now holding more interest than sliding, she hadn't quite yet put all her interest in childish things away, and decided she wanted to give the saucer a try.

Believing herself too old to ride with the "little kids", and ignoring our warning about the tendency of the saucer to go faster with less weight, she insisted on going alone. We set her off with a push that I have to admit, may have been a bit harder than strictly necessary, and she flew down the hill, picking up speed as predicted. Upon reaching the bottom of the run, instead of being stopped by the old fence, she rocketed right through it and, with pickets flying in all directions, sailed straight across the road and over the breastwork. Luckily, the tide was up, so when the saucer hit the water, it skipped a couple of times, then came to a stop and slowly sank under her.

Drenched to the neck, the distraught young lady waded back to shore, thoughtfully dragging the saucer behind her, and swearing a blue streak. She had a memorable ride, but I'm afraid her hairdo and makeup were ruined.

One snowy evening a couple of years later, I was hanging onto a rope tied to the back of Barry Morton's car, and was being pulled along the Front Road in the saucer. There was quite a fierce storm going on, and we expected the roads to be pretty much deserted, but, just in front of the Co-Op Store, we suddenly met oncoming traffic.

The saucer had been zigzagging back and forth across the road, so I pulled on the rope to swing myself in behind Barry's back bumper as the other car passed. My timing must have been off slightly, because I swung back out again, right in front of Dick Thompson's station wagon. Seeing that a collision was unavoidable, I hung on to the rope and started to stand up.

The front of the car struck me, and the rope that I was still clutching pulled me across the hood, so I landed on the road beside the car. I don't know who was more startled and scared, me or Dick.

I spent the next couple of days in bed with a badly bruised hip, but the real victim of this fiasco was the saucer. It ended up under Dick's front wheel, bent and twisted, its sliding days forever over. Someone dragged it out from under the car and unceremoniously dumped it over the breastwork onto the beach, a sad and inglorious end to a great instrument of winter fun.

**Ben Robicheau**

## 14: Movie night

Playing outside was not our only source of entertainment. If we got tired of climbing the breastwork, bobsledding through traffic, riding our bikes, or getting run down in flying saucers, there was always the option, at least for one night of the week, of going to the movies.

Nowadays, if anyone mentions movie night, they are most likely talking about an evening slouched on the living-room couch in front of a flat-screen TV with a bag of microwave popcorn and a Netflix membership. Not so long ago, a night at the movies meant something a little grander. It was more of a community social event, a chance to dress up a bit and go out to the local cinema, where you might meet up with family, friends, and neighbours, and spend a couple of hours lost together in a big-screen adventure.

Almost every town in those days had a movie theatre, and for many people taking in the latest film was a regular event. Even small communities, like the ones on the Islands, had theatres. Bernard Gower and Holland Titus built the one in Westport, but by the time I became aware of it in the fifties, Gerald Strickland owned it. The official name of the theatre was 'The Star' although I don't think many people were aware of this fact, since I have never heard it referred to as anything other than "Gerald's Hall".

Since it was located right next to the school, more or less where the fire hall is now, the theatre was a familiar building to us kids. Because the 155-seat wooden structure was built on posts with a slant from front to back to accommodate the sloping floor, the front part of the building was about four feet off the ground. This provided a handy shelter for the younger students to go under to get out of the weather while waiting for the schoolhouse doors to open; and for some of the older students, it was a place safely off school property where they could discreetly take their recess smoke break.

Although I was well acquainted with the outside of the building from an early age, I didn't get to see the inside until I was ten years old. Since Saturday night was the only night the theatre was open, and my father had to work in his store every Saturday night, we had never been able to go to a movie as a family.

I don't recall if it was my idea or my father's, but I do remember the excitement I felt when he presented me with thirty-five cents one Saturday night, and told me I was now old enough to go to the movie by myself. Since it would be dark by the time the movie was over, he also gave me a flashlight to help me avoid the mud puddles on my way home.

I felt quite grown up as I joined the dozen or so other movie patrons on the high steps in front of the theatre doors. We must have been a bit early, be-

## Two Ferries Out

cause while we were standing there, expecting the doors to open any moment, Mr. Strickland came walking down the Back Road with the round metal can containing this evening's 16mm film tucked under his arm. After making his way through the scant crowd to unlock the door, he then kept us waiting for another fifteen minutes or so while he set up the film and made the necessary technical preparations.

Finally, the doors were flung open, and our small group of theatre-goers filed in to see Gerald sitting in a little booth with a roll of tickets in his hand and a display of potato chips and chocolate bars laid out beside him.

Admission turned out to be twenty-five cents, which left me with a dilemma; did I spend my extra dime on two bags of Scottie's chips at a nickel each or one chocolate bar at eight cents? I decided on the chips.

I cautiously made my way into the auditorium juggling my two bags of chips; my theatre ticket; which I thought I had to keep ready in case someone —I don't know who—asked to see it; the flashlight; and my winter coat. I had just got settled in my seat and organized all my items, when it happened: that thrilling moment when the houselights dim and the projector beam hits the silver screen.

Unfortunately, I don't remember a whole lot about the movie other than that it was a western of some sort. Just as the image of galloping horses hit the screen, I dropped my flashlight on the floor and it somehow came on! I quickly grabbed it up from where it had rolled under the seat in front of me and tried to turn it off, but it wouldn't turn off!

After a couple of minutes of fiddling with the switch, all the while trying to ignore mounting complaints about the distracting light from those around me, I gave up on turning it off, and attempted to hide it by shoving it in my pants pocket. This turned out to be very uncomfortable, plus I felt a little conspicuous sitting there with the front of my pants glowing, so I just wrapped it up in my coat and placed it on the seat beside me.

Just as I was starting to get interested in the movie, the flashlight fell off the seat again and rolled down the floor for a second time, splashing light all over the auditorium and onto the screen! I quickly retrieved it and wrapped it up again. Over the next half-hour or so, I spent more time fussing with the flashlight and worrying about disrupting the movie than actually watching what was on the screen. In the end I resolved the problem by taking the flashlight apart and putting the pieces in my pockets. Again, this was kind of uncomfortable, but at least this time my pants weren't lit up!

By the time the movie finally ended, night had fallen, and after unsuccessfully trying to figure out how to put the flashlight back together, I ended up walking home in the pitch dark, clinking and rattling along with my pockets full of batteries and flashlight bits and pieces, and trying to avoid stepping in the unseen mud puddles.

**Two Ferries Out**

This memorable event turned out to be my one and only visit to the Westport movie theatre. TV had recently arrived on the Island, and within the next few months, attendance at the theatre rapidly dropped off to the point where it was no longer feasible to stay open. The building was used for storage for a few years, and eventually was torn down to make way for the new fire hall.

Luckily for those of us interested in the cinematic arts, over in Freeport, Lloyd Blackford, having a bigger population to draw from, managed to keep The Nu-Era Theatre going for a few more years. When I was thirteen or so, I went to a Jerry Lewis movie there with my friend Jimmy.

The Nu-Era was bigger and fancier than the Westport theatre; it ran the professional-quality 35mm films, could seat 200 patrons, had a stage in front of the screen for live performances, and even had balcony seating. In fact, since several people had warned me not to sit right below the balcony because of the tendency of people to "accidentally" spill drinks and drop various items over the edge onto the customers below, we decided it was probably safer to watch the show from the second level seats.

Again, this was the only opportunity I would have to attend a movie in this theatre. Sometime in the early sixties, it too closed, although the attached dance hall would continue on for several more years. Unlike the now long-gone Westport theatre building, Lloyd's Hall still survives: The Royal Canadian Le-

**Ben Robicheau**

gion bought it in the 70s and it lives on today as the Carpiquet Branch #92.

A few years after the Freeport theatre closed, someone at Islands Consolidated School came up with the idea of starting a Cinema Club. They would put on one movie a month for the public and with luck make some money for the Student Council.

The first presentation was to be the classic Steve McQueen movie, *Bullitt.* On the big night, there was a pretty good turn-out, most of the stackable plastic chairs in the school auditorium were filled, and the canteen was doing a brisk business, everything was looking good, maybe the novelty of the TV tube had worn off by now, and people were interested in going out to the movies again...Then the film started, and it all went downhill.

I don't know if the problem was with the poor condition of the 16mm film the distributor had sent us, the inexperience of the volunteer projectionist, or the school's rickety old Bell & Howell projector—probably a combination of all three—but just a few minutes into the movie, the film jammed up, and the lights had to be brought up while it was fixed. The problem was quickly rectified, the lights dimmed again, and the film continued. A few minutes later, another jam, lights up again, short delay, lights down.

This continued on an annoyingly regular basis throughout the rest of the film, the projector continuously jamming every few minutes, and the lights going on and off like a slow-motion strobe light.

## Two Ferries Out

Among film buffs, *Bullitt* is considered to contain one of the most exciting and suspenseful car chase scenes in movie history. Unfortunately for the audience that night, having it interrupted every few minutes made it very hard to appreciate the drama.

The I.C.S. student's council screened a few more movies in the following months, and although they went off quite smoothly in comparison, the audience, maybe turned off by their initial experience, quickly dwindled, and the Cinema Club was forced to quietly follow in the footsteps of the Star and the Nu-Era, bringing to a final close the era of film on the Islands.

**Ben Robicheau**

## 15: TV time

When the local movie house became a thing of the past, most islanders turned for entertainment to the very thing that had helped kill it. There is no doubt that today's television-watching can be quite a technical affair, what with coffee tables around the country collapsing under the weight of the many remote controls needed to operate our digital this, and hi-def that, our VCRs, DVDs, surround sound systems, satellite receivers, video games and streaming boxes. But there was a time when an evening of television watching required a set of technical skills quite different from knowing which button to push on which remote.

I can (just barely) remember a time when there were no TVs at all. I'm not sure who had the first set on Brier Island, but I can recall the excitement caused by the fact that someone we knew actually had one of these amazing, futuristic gizmos that we had, up to now, only read about in *Life* magazine or *Popular Mechanics*.

The first few people to get TV sets suddenly found themselves at the centre of the Island's social scene. Neighbours would drop by after supper, and spend the evening staring at the snowy images on the small black and white screen. Not that there was a whole lot to look at in the beginning. Programming didn't start until late in the afternoon; up until then, all there was to see was the "test pattern" which, for some reason, was the profile of an Indian chief centred in a bulls-eye. Still, people would sit and stare at the test pattern, thrilled to see any image at all. At midnight, the National Anthem would play and your programming day would conclude.

At first, there was just one station: CHSJ from Saint John, NB. A couple of years later, we could pick up a second channel from the Yarmouth area. To receive these channels, you needed an antenna. These antennas were usually mounted on the end of a long wooden pole or metal pipe, the higher the better. You rotated this pipe slowly until the antenna detected the station signal and an image materialized through the snow on the TV screen.

Aiming the antenna was a delicate procedure, accomplished with much yelling back and forth between the antenna adjuster, on the roof, and someone inside watching the TV. "Okay, Okay you've got it, oh, you went too far, go back, no, too far back, Okay, right there, that's good". Once you attained maximum picture quality, the antenna adjuster locked the antenna in place. When the Yarmouth station was added, you had to either go out and rotate the antenna every time you wanted to change the channel, or install a second antenna and a switch so you could just flip from one antenna to the other as you changed the channel dial.

Of course, every time we got a big wind storm, most of the antennas on the Island would move slightly, and then have to be adjusted again. Our antenna was on a long steel pipe located conveniently right by the living room window, so all you had to do was go outside with a pipe wrench, look in the window at the TV, and crank the pipe around until you had a good picture. Some people tried to avoid weather problems altogether by putting their antennas in the attic, but usually the signal wasn't as strong as it was with an outside antenna.

Occasionally, the weather would be the TV watcher's friend. If a hurricane was imminent, the unusual weather conditions could sometimes make it possible to pick up a few of the Maine Coast stations. Although it was very exciting to be able to watch programs we didn't usually get to see, this phenomenon would usually last only a few hours until the storm arrived in full force, and it would, of course, then knock your antenna out of kilter so you'd have no TV at all!

In very short order, the TV set held pride of place in nearly every living room, bringing in black and white images from around the world. Then came the next big advance, colour! The first colour TVs were expensive, and, of course, everyone already had a perfectly good black and white set, so it was hard to justify buying an expensive new colour one. But there was a way to supposedly get around this. My father came home one day with a sheet of plastic that you could stick to the screen, and it would magically transform your dreary old black and white TV into a modern colour set. The sheet was made up of tiny prisms, and if you looked at it from different angles, you could see red, blue and green, but these colours didn't necessarily conform to the picture behind it. You did have colour, but it was just randomly spread across the screen. There was another "instant colour" system that was also a plastic sheet that was put in front of the TV, with this, the bottom section was tinted green, it was a sort of amber colour in the middle, and blue on the top. If you were looking at scenery it gave the impression of green grass and blue sky, but it didn't really work for anything else; people always looked like they were wearing green shirts and had blue hair!

The first actual colour sets were extremely temperamental. After you set up your new TV in the corner, or in whichever part of the living room you chose, you would have to call Edgar McDormand to come and tune it in. He would arrive with his toolbox of special TV-tuning tools, and then spend half the day hunched down between the TV and the wall, adjusting and fine-tuning until the colour was acceptable. If you decided later on to move the set to a different place in the room, everything would be thrown out of whack, and he would have to come back again to re-tune it.

Edgar was also the man to call when your TV broke down. If the picture wouldn't stop rolling, or people's faces were a kind of sickly purple-green, or the picture was squeezed down to a two-inch strip in the middle of the screen, he would show up with his suitcase full of glass vacuum tubes and spend the

## Two Ferries Out

next hour or so switching out various tubes until trial-and-error narrowed it down to the one that was causing the problem.

Once you got your TV working right again, it was time to watch some shows! By the mid-sixties, Saturday night's *Hockey Night In Canada* was a must-see for sports fans; but for the rest of us, Sunday night was prime TV watching time. Right after supper, there was *Walt Disney* for the kids, then there was something for everyone on *The Ed Sullivan Show;* remember Topo Gigio with his "Kees mee Eddieee"? After the kids went to bed, it was time to join the Cartwright boys for some Western adventures on *Bonanza*.

One show that was popular in our house, and I'm sure in the whole area, was *Time For Juniors*. This was a kind of early, low-key, East Coast version of *Canadian Idol*. Produced in Saint John, it featured local children showing off their talents; or, in some cases, lack of talent. The host, Jeanie Wood, was something of a celebrity in the Maritimes. I remember a woman from Westport who made a trip across the Bay to visit relatives in Saint John. Upon her return, all she could talk about was that she had met Jeanie Wood on *The Princess Helene*.

There is no doubt that the arrival of television changed Island life; some would say for the better, and others might argue that it was for the worse. Today many of the shows and events that we watched unfold on those snowy screens are considered important pieces of our social and cultural history. When I was about nine years old, I myself played a very small and generally unknown role in the history of television on Brier Island.

Before we even had a TV at home, my father installed one in the store. TVs were still rare on the Island at this time, and I guess the idea was that it would attract customers. It was a big floor model in a wooden cabinet that sat on four skinny legs. To raise it up so that people could see it, Dad put it on top of an old iron safe that stood next to, and was about level with, the ice cream freezer. The four legs just fit on the very corners of the safe.

One evening, a few weeks after it was installed, a crowd of men were watching the hockey game when I dropped by for an ice cream sandwich. The ice cream freezer was the old style with hatches on the top; to get your ice cream, you had to fold back the hatch cover and reach down in.

On this fateful night, the freezer was nearly empty, and I had to really stretch to the bottom for that ice cream. I couldn't quite reach it, and with my head and one arm in the freezer, I groped around with my other arm for something to boost myself up a bit more. My free hand found a convenient grip and I used the leverage to pull myself up another couple of inches until I could reach the object of my efforts.

Just as my hand closed on the elusive Ice cream sandwich, I heard a collective roar from the assembled crowd, followed immediately by a resounding crash.

With a feeling of dread, I pulled my head out of the freezer and turned, ice cream sandwich in hand, to see the TV lying on the floor behind me in a heap of broken wood, shattered glass, and sparking innards. My grip had been on the leg of the TV, and when I pulled myself up, I pulled the leg over the edge of the safe, and down went the TV.

My desire for a frozen treat had unwittingly catapulted me into the dubious position of being the first person on Brier Island to totally destroy a television set!

**Ben Robicheau**

*Dune jumping at Pond Cove*

## 16: Family day

Playtime was a luxury almost entirely reserved for us kids. Most of the adults in the village worked at physically-demanding jobs, so leisure time for them could be a rare and precious commodity. Public leisure time for most adults consisted of attending community events with their families. School and church events, like Christmas concerts and graduations were usually well-attended, and one of the most popular events was the annual Sunday school picnic, where we got to see our friend's parents in a different light, competing in the three-legged race, hopping across the field in the sack race, tossing bean bags, or playing the part of the wheelbarrow in the wheelbarrow race.

In our family, Sunday was usually the only day when we got to do something all together. Dad worked in his fish business five and a half days a week (they only worked until noon on Saturday), and he also worked Monday to Saturday evenings in the store, so that left only one day for family activities.

Since all the stores on the island were closed on Sunday, it was not unusual for someone to come knocking on our door, asking if Dad could 'Just run to the store for a minute'. Sometimes it was a true emergency, to get medicine for a sick child or gas for an unexpected trip to Digby, but, more often than not, it was because someone had run out of cigarettes or they were in desperate need of pop and chips. Therefore, our Sundays usually included an outing of some sort that would put us out of reach for a few hours.

Mostly, our family outings involved going for a drive—sometimes just around the Island to see the sights, sometimes to the lighthouse or Pond Cove or Scataway Cove for a wiener roast or picnic. We seemed to go on a lot of picnics...I guess it was an economical way to entertain and feed a family of nine kids.

One of the picnic spots we went to was on a piece of land my father owned, half-way down Western Light Road. The part nearest the road was a sort of gravel pit, but in behind there was a woodlot where Dad used to cut firewood. In a small clearing among the trees he had built a little picnic area, complete with a fire pit, a swing, a teeter-totter, and a picnic table made out of boards and logs. On days when the beach was too cold or windy or foggy (sometimes all three at once), our drives would often end up here, as it was often quite warm and fog-free in this protected spot in the middle of the island.

One Sunday, we set out specifically to visit our forest picnic spot. We hiked in, loaded down with hot dogs and marshmallows and various other picnic goodies. After some time spent swinging and teetering and running around gathering up twigs and

## Two Ferries Out

sticks for the fire, we were ready to start roasting some hot dogs.

Then Dad discovered that he had forgotten the matches. To hike back out and drive home for matches would take a lot longer than we hungry, hot dog craving, kids could bear, so Dad came up with a solution to our problem. He had carried the supplies in an old orange crate which was made out of some type of light, thin wood, he broke off a couple of slats of this wood and began rubbing them together.

Now, I had seen Tonto make fire like this for The Lone Ranger dozens of times on TV, but I had never actually seen it done in real life, and I wasn't sure it could actually be done; maybe it was one of those things that only happened in the movies, like cowboys shooting ten shots from a six-shooter or playing guitar while riding their horse, or rough-and-tumble cowboys singing a song at the end of every adventure.

After several minutes of trying to produce fire with friction, the only thing heating up was Dad. The beads of sweat were standing out on his forehead, and I was thinking that unless Tonto showed up, we weren't going to be roasting anything today, when suddenly a wisp of smoke curled up from the piece of orange crate under his hand. He increased his efforts, and now I could see a tiny glowing spot on the wood. With a little gentle blowing and the addition of bits of dried moss and some shredded birch bark, the glowing ember soon burst into flame, and within seconds, we had a real fire going. I was very impressed, and spent the rest of the day thinking that I now had something in common with The Lone Ranger.

Not all of our Sunday drives were restricted to the Island. We sometimes ventured up the Neck to take a dip in the usually frigid waters of Lake Midway, or maybe all the way out to South Range and Porters Lake, where a couple of friends had cottages where we could enjoy the exotic experience of playing in water that didn't turn you blue after five minutes.

Occasionally, Dad would combine business with pleasure, load up the truck with kids and fish, and head up the Valley to do some trading for apples, berries or whatever was in season (he just traded the fish, not the kids).

For many years, a truck was the only vehicle we had, so except for the two youngest, who got to ride in the cab, all us kids rode in the back. On long trips, it wasn't all that comfortable, although we did have the luxury of an old tarp for protection in case of rain or snow. It also tended to get kind of boring back there. looking at where we had been, instead of where we were going. We passed the time by trying to get the people in the car behind us to wave back, or by thinking up other ways to entertain ourselves. On one occasion, we were on our way back home down Digby Neck, when Dad became a bit annoyed after he glanced in the rear-view mirror and noticed that we were pelting mailboxes with the apples he had just traded his salt fish for.

## Two Ferries Out

In June of 1960, we left home for a family trip up the Valley. We travelled through Digby and Annapolis Royal, crossing over the Annapolis River on the bridge to Granville Ferry. That afternoon we were on our way back home and stopped at a roadside park just past Bridgetown for a bite to eat (another picnic). My father got chatting with some other people in the park, and when they heard we were heading toward Digby, they told us we wouldn't be able to get there on this road because the Granville bridge was gone. Apparently, not long after we crossed it, the bridge had suddenly collapsed into the river. I remember feeling cut off from home and stranded at hearing this news. I guess I thought the bridge was like a ferry: if it wasn't working, you were stuck where you were. Of course, all we had to do was backtrack to Bridgetown and cross over the river there.

Another Sunday pastime we used to enjoy was going for hikes along the shore. On one of our walks, Dad invited Sidney Melanson along. Sydney was from the Meteghan area and worked for Dad in the fishplant. He was a good worker but wasn't the type to look at any form of exercise as entertainment. However, on this day he agreed to come along, and we set out for Pond Cove.

The plan was to walk across the pond wall, a narrow strip of rock and sand that wave action had formed between the beach and the Big and Little Ponds. Ordinarily, it would be a fairly easy walk along this narrow strip, but we were in late September, it was almost high tide, and there was a strong wind blowing with big rollers breaking onshore.

Hiking across this wall in front of Big Pond, we were able to stay back a reasonable distance from the water, and, except for the occasional scattering of light spray, all went well. The pond wall in front of Little Pond was a lot narrower and closer to the water, and here we ran into a bit of a problem. By the time we got to this section of our hike, the tide had risen further up the beach and the waves were breaking right over the wall into the pond.

We considered turning around, but by now it was nearly as bad behind us, plus it was farther to go back than forward. After hunkering down in the shelter of a big log for a while, Dad noticed that only every third wave was big enough to come right over the wall, if we timed it right, we should be able to run across in the gap between the big waves. Dad would go first, then Sydney and I would go together.

Even though Sydney expressed some doubt about this plan, as soon as the next big wave withdrew, Dad took off running and made it to the other side just before the next big breaker hit. Now it was our turn. I counted off the three waves, and then made my dash, with Sydney right behind me. Part way across, he decided he wasn't going to be able make it, and turned back. I got to the other side just in time to see him disappear behind a wall of foaming spray.

When all had cleared, Sydney was nowhere to be seen, and we were starting to think maybe he had been swept out to sea, when his head popped up from behind the log. He was soaked, but safe. But now he wasn't going to move from that log. Nothing, no amount of encouragement, no shouted explanation, no yelling to "Just do it" was going to convince him. Finally, Dad had to run back and get him. It wasn't all that dangerous, it was just a matter of timing, but Sydney was convinced that he had barely escaped with his life.

That was the last time we went hiking with Sydney, or, rather, he went hiking with us. For some reason, he never again took us up on an invitation to join one of our Sunday excursions.

**Ben Robicheau**

*Working on my '56 Chev*

## 17: California dreamin'

As I got older, my taste in pastimes changed somewhat. The arrival of TV had exposed me to political and social changes in the wider world, and I was reading about important happenings in other places. And the radio that provided a near-constant soundtrack to our teen-age lives kept me constantly informed of important, up-to-the-minute, world-shaking events.

I became a teenager at the beginning of the 1960s. I spent most of these formative years listening to the evolution of Rock and Roll music as broadcast across the Gulf of Maine by disc jockeys like Arnie "Woo-Woo" Ginsburg of Boston radio station WMEX. The airwaves of the time were dominated by U.S. West Coast groups like The Beach Boys and Jan and Dean singing songs about sun, surf, girls and cars. Songs like *Surf City, Surfin' Safari, Little Deuce Coupe, Drag City, Little G.T.O.* and *California Girls* painted an alluring picture of a lifestyle that we on the East Coast of Canada could only dream of. In December of 1965, The Mamas and the Papas came out with the song *California Dreamin'*. Many of us here in the frozen north could identify with the lines "California dreamin', On a winter's day"...plus, a member of that band was Denny Doherty from Halifax, so we practically had a personal connection to the custom-car-driving, surfboard-riding, flower-power world of the West Coast.

In our minds, every guy in California spent endless sunny days cruising around in a fast car with a hot chick by his side and a surfboard strapped to the roof. He was always on the way to Malibu or Topanga Beach to catch some wild surf, or cruising Deadman's Curve on the lookout for a chance to drag race some other surfer with an equally hot car and hot chick.

Here on Brier Island, my friends and I did our best to copy what we thought was the California lifestyle. After all, we lived on a coast, we were surrounded by the sea, we had beaches. It was really not all that different from being in California, if you overlooked the fact that, on many days, the sun was barely visible through the fog, and if you tried to ignore the total absence of both surfing opportunities and endless highways for driving and racing. We tried hard to convince ourselves that we, too, could live the hot-rod surfer life; but to be truthful, the severe shortage of endless summers, cool cars and sun-tanned, bikini-wearing, blonde-haired beach babes really made it difficult to accurately emulate those laid-back surfer dudes.

Still, we did the best we could with what we had. We tried to copy the surfer look by cutting the legs off of perfectly good pants to make surfing shorts. These were called "baggies" and we wore them faithfully, even when our knees turned blue from the cold. We even tried to make a surfboard out of some

## Two Ferries Out

scrap plywood and almost froze our baggies off in a less-than-successful attempt to surf at Pond Cove. Since the board couldn't really support us, and the waves were nowhere close to being big enough to ride on anyway, our surfin' safari wasn't all that successful. The best we could do, was to float the board in the water near the shore, then run down the beach, jump on it, and skid out ten or fifteen feet before sinking in the ice-cold water.

We eventually came to the realization that our island was not well-equipped to allow us to follow the surfer's life. We did sometimes get big surf on the islands, but it was almost always during hurricanes and winter storms; not the best time to hit the beach. We came to the reluctant, but obvious conclusion, that we were not going to become surfer dudes, so we turned our attention to another important aspect of teenage life, cars.

We might not have surf, but we did have cars. Sure, we didn't have the bored and stroked, chopped and channelled, metal-flake painted, tire-smoking, screamin' machines that we pored over in the pages of *Hot Rod Magazine*, but the cars we did have had one advantage: they were cheap.

Ricky and Wayne went in together on one of these bargain automobiles, investing $12.50 each in an old Chev that had been sitting in Dick Thompson's yard for several years. They soon decided their new ride would look better as a convertible, and using high-tech tools like an axe, a hacksaw, and a sledgehammer, went to work "customizing" it. The roof came off OK, but they didn't stop there. By the time the job was done, all that remained of the body was the front fenders, windshield, front doors and front seat. A rope across the back of the seat tied the doors together to keep them shut.

This Island version of a California Hot Rod lasted less than a week. One afternoon they stopped to ask if I wanted to go for a ride. The only seat was already crammed full with four people, so I would have to crouch down on the floor behind and hang on to the door rope.

I decided to pass on their offer, a good decision as it turned out, because about twenty minutes later they flipped the car on Pea Jack Road. Two riders were thrown clear and the other two were able to duck down in the seat as the car rolled completely upside down on top of them. Except for a bit of road rash and a few bumps and scrapes, all escaped unharmed.

The summer he was seventeen, my friend Leonard got a job in one of the fishplants. He decided that the most fiscally responsible thing he could do with his first paycheque was to invest it in the purchase of an old car. Luckily for him, Weymouth Motors had placed an ad in *The Digby Courier* that week, offering terrific deals on a variety of used cars in what we were led to believe was near-perfect condition. One of these excellent vehicles, a twenty-year-old Pontiac, was on sale for the unbelievably low price of only ninety-nine dollars. Leonard didn't yet have a driver's licence, so he asked if I would hitchhike with him to Weymouth and drive his new car home.

We arrived at Weymouth Motors and found his car sitting dejectedly at the back of the lot with two flat tires. After pumping up the tires and a bit of tinkering by the mechanic to boost the dead battery, and then more tinkering to get the engine started, we were finally ready to hit the road for home.

This turned out to be easier said than done. To get out of the town of Weymouth, you had to cross a one-lane bridge and then immediately go up a steep hill. Half-way up the hill, our car gradually came to a stop; it didn't have the power to go any farther. We turned around and went back to the garage, where they told us the engine hadn't been run for quite a while and it probably just needed to warm up a bit more to unleash the full power of that six-cylinder, flathead engine.

We spent the next hour trying to get out of town. We tried going as far up the hill in the opposite direction as we could, then turning around and bombing through town as fast as we dared to go, weaving through traffic and dodging pedestrians. If we were lucky, we wouldn't have to stop for someone coming across the bridge and we could get a running shot at the hill.

We made several failed attempts. Then, finally, it looked like we were actually going to make it. We managed a fast, unobstructed dash down the opposing hill and through the main business district, found the bridge clear of traffic, bombed across at what for the old Pontiac was close to top speed, and roared up the, until now, insurmountable hill.

Thanks to timing everything just right, and a bit of good luck, we were about to finally achieve our objective when, just before the crest of the hill, the car in front of us stopped for a train that chose just that moment to cross the road.

We had no choice but to stop with the rest of the traffic. When the train had passed and the other cars finally pulled away, there we were, left sitting mere feet from the top without the power to get going again.

We headed back to the garage one more time, and managed to convince them that there was definitely something wrong with the car. They told us to leave it for a few days and they'd take a look at it. We hitch-hiked home and returned a week later to find that the problem had been a cracked distributor cap. This time we roared up the hill with no trouble at all.

My own first car was a 1956 Chev. On rainy days you had to watch out for water and mud flying up through the holes in the floor, and everywhere I went a thick cloud of oily smoke followed me because the worn-out engine burned almost as much oil as it did gas, but I thought after my father talked the seller down from seventy-five to sixty-five dollars that we had got a great bargain.

I eventually was able to eliminate its two major problems by installing a plywood floor and rebuilding the engine myself. I didn't really know what I was doing with the engine, so I'd work along until I got stuck, then go ask Ace McDormand or one of the other local self-taught mechanics what to do next. It took me a couple of months but, surprisingly, when I eventually got it all back together, it actually ran!

In those days, annual mechanical inspections were not required, and even insurance was not mandatory. Once you paid for the car, your only other expenses were gas and registration, and there were ways around both of those.

If you stayed on the island, you could get away without license plates or even a driver's license. The RCMP were stationed in Digby, only forty miles away, but they rarely visited the islands; and when they did, there was only one way on and off, so as soon as they appeared at the first ferry, people would put to use the Citizens Band radios that were popular in many boats, cars, and homes at the time to raise the alarm, resulting in any less-than-legitimate vehicles magically disappearing from sight by the time the police drove off the ferry.

I'm sure a lot of people weren't too happy about us unlicensed drivers cruising around the island in our unregistered, uninsured, mechanically-suspect cars, but we saw all that paperwork as a lot of unnecessary hassle and expense. You could even reduce the cost of putting gas in your car somewhat by using the tax-free dyed gas that the fishermen used in their boats. It was cheaper than regular gas, but also illegal to use in anything but a fishing boat. There was a "gas inspector" who would arrive periodically to take test samples from vehicles' gas tanks and issue a big fine if you were caught with "marked" gas; but, as with the police, the Island's early-warning system usually alerted us about their imminent arrival.

The Beach Boys and the Mamas and the Papas didn't have the ice-cold Bay of Fundy water, the seaweed-covered beach of Pond Cove, or chopped-up old cars in mind when they sang their songs glorifying the California lifestyle, and I imagine they would have gotten a good laugh out of our attempts to copy what we thought was the daily life of the West Coast teenager; but, looking back on it now, we did have a lot of fun and freedom and, in a way, developed our own unique coastal lifestyle.

## 18: The working life

The cars and motorcycles my friends and I were now interested in were proving a more expensive hobby, and required a lot more upkeep, than the sleds and bicycles of our younger years. Up until this point, the first days of summer marked the end of the trials and tribulations of the school year. Exams were over, report cards were finally in our hands, for better or worse, and two solid months of idle freedom stretched out in front of us. For years, summer vacation had consisted of endless days of taking it easy: sleeping in, hiking to the back shore, riding your bike to Pond Cove, messing around on the beach, berry picking; doing pretty well whatever you wanted, whenever you wanted. But, like all good things, this idyllic existence eventually came to an end. By our mid-teens, the pursuit of freedom required your own set of wheels, or at least the ability to put gas in your parents' car. This required money, and that required a summer job.

On the Islands, summer employment opportunities were somewhat limited; but there were still a few possibilities, starting with the traditional kid jobs, like babysitting and lawn mowing. Herb Barnaby recalls a couple of summers when he had built up a mowing empire of over forty lawns, fetching the princely sum of two dollars per lawn. Peggy

Thompson, Janice Albright, Heather Williamson and Brenda McDormand managed to land much-sought-after jobs at a little hamburger joint called Foof's Place, serving up burgers and milkshakes to the rest of us who were eagerly spending our babysitting and lawn-cutting money.

An occasional source of summer employment for a few was the Highways Department. My sister Janet remembers having "so much fun" the summer she and sister Ruth Ellen, along with Betty Ann McDormand and Reta Barnaby, were hired to cut the brush along the side of the road.

In those low-tech days, before they had tractor-mounted Bushhogs to efficiently mangle and shred the roadside shrubbery, the bushes, tall grass and weeds were cut by hand, a laborious, but much more environmentally friendly and esthetically pleasing method which usually produced a nice, neat job, and several weeks of reasonably well-paid work for a few students.

Periwinkling was another way to pick up a bit of money. Periwinkles, or 'pennywinkles' as they were called locally, were plentiful on the rocks around the island, but you could only pick winkles when the tide was down. Although the work was hard on the back, the pay for a bucket of winkles made it worthwhile; and it was a job you could do after school and on weekends year-round.

For several years my father provided a demand for these sea snails that both kids and adults in need of a little quick pocket money filled. The winkles were bagged and shipped live to the States where, apparently, they were popular snacks in bars around the Boston area, a sort of poor man's escargot. Dad's winkle-exporting business was even featured on CBC's "Land and Sea" in an episode called "The Periwinkle King".

For younger kids with an entrepreneurial bent, there were the traditional Kool-Aid stands or the ever-popular roadside sales of coloured glass, rocks and shells collected from the beach. One summer, a couple of my sisters sold painted scallop shells door-to-door for "Ten cents apiece, or two for a quarter". They were puzzled that some people seemed reluctant to take advantage of the two-shell deal.

Starting around age fourteen or so, if you were a member of a fishing family, you were pretty well guaranteed a job for the summer. In fact, for some, a summer job working on their father's boat turned into a permanent situation. Every fall, someone would not return to school, deciding his future lay more with hooks than with books.

The fishery was by far the biggest employer on the Islands, and for many years, the numerous fish-processing facilities were a reliable source of steady employment. The larger facilities, like Connors Brothers, located next to the ferry slip in Freeport, were referred to as "fish factories", the more numerous but smaller establishments were called "fishplants".

The summer I was fourteen, I went to work in my father's fishplant. Of course, I had been around the place my whole life, and so thought I was quite familiar with what went on there. My first day on the job I found out that I still had a lot to learn.

*My father's fishplant, including the 'buckman'.*

At eight o'clock on a cold, foggy morning, I found myself standing at a keeler, the wooden bin which was the fish's first stop in its journey through the plant, decked out in my new barvel, a rubber apron which offered a modicum of protection from flying fish guts, among other things. I was going to spend my summer gutting fish.

The system of commercial fish processing at our plant started when the small local boats, mostly hand liners, came in alongside a narrow wooden ramp to "sell out". This ramp extended out from the end of the building down into the water. It consisted of wooden "rails" on each side with a board walkway in between. This walkway had slats nailed across it every ten or so inches to provide traction; still, it was very slippery to walk on when wet, especially the

## Two Ferries Out

lower part of the ramp which spent more time under water, and was covered in moss and seaweed.

The purpose of the parallel wooden rails was to act as a track for the cart that collected the fish. The cart was a big wooden box on four steel wheels which was lowered down the ramp by gravity, and then drawn back up again by a steel cable wrapped around the drum of a large electric winch.

The fishermen pitched-forked their fish into the cart. It was then winched back up into the shed, and a door in the side of the cart was opened. The sloping bottom of the cart funnelled the fish out onto the floor, where workers sorted them by species, weighed them, and ferried them via an overhead track system across the room to be dumped into the "keeler" to be gutted and headed.

This cart was sturdily built, and by itself weighed several hundred pounds. Loaded with fish, the weight could be up to two or three thousand pounds. When Dad first went into the fish-buying business, he tried to economize by using rope to draw up the cart instead of a steel cable. The very first load he pulled only made it half-way up the ramp before the rope broke and the cart rocketed back down the ramp and into the water. The fisherman had to go gather all his fish back again, as well as the cart.

Right around the time I started working, a different style of fishing with bigger boats known as draggers became popular. Dad built a wharf extension out into deeper water so the draggers could get in to unload at any time of tide. This extension consisted of a hoisting shed built on a cribwork of logs, and an abutment or, as my younger sisters called it, a 'buckman'. From this buckman a steel barrel was lowered on a cable to collect the fish. Since the fishermen were paid a different price for different species of fish, they put only one species at a time in the barrel. The barrel-load was then weighed and transported via a sluice system to the shed where the fish were dumped directly into the keelers, or into holding tanks if the keelers were full.

This system required less physical effort and caused less damage to the fish than the old, more pitchfork-intensive, method, but it used water pumped straight from the harbour to move the fish along, making it rather uncomfortable for the workers at the end of the sluice, who spent most of the day standing on a concrete floor awash in very cold ocean water. This was where I was positioned for my first job "working in the fish".

As the sluice dumped the fish at my station, the first person, the 'throater' would grab one out of the steadily mounting pile. Placing his thumb under the jaw and index finger in an eye, he flipped it backwards over the edge of the keeler and cut across the throat. Next, he would run his knife down the belly. A second cut across the throat would sever the spine and remove the head.

The fish would then pass on to the next person, the 'gutter'. This was the lowest and least prestigious position at the keeler. This was my job. After I pulled out the intestines, the fish, at this point called a 'round fish', went right from the keeler to the splitting table.

The splitter could be considered the maestro of the fish plant. It takes a certain amount of skill, stamina, and maybe you could even call it artistry, to properly split a fish. The splitting knife was a unique instrument, it had a wide, square-ended blade with a twist to it. Your job as a splitter was to remove the backbone by slicing down both sides of it, severing the ribs as it went, then chopping through the spine near the tail and pulling up one end of the spine and cutting underneath as you work your way back to the head, thus completely removing the backbone. You then pushed the split fish off the table to be rinsed in the splitting tub, a large barrel of constantly-flushing salt water.

Although accomplished in mere seconds, this procedure was harder than it looked, and required much more finesse than described here. Cut too deep and you could go through the skin and ruin the fish; not deep enough and it was a time-wasting struggle to get the backbone out and the de-boned fish might not lie flat.

A well-split fish would lie perfectly open, flat on the table. These 'flat fish' would then be pitchforked out of the splitting tub into a box suspended from an overhead track system, then wheeled off to be salted. They would be laid out in layers, neatly stacked like bundles of shingles, in square, watertight bins called salt tanks. Coarse rock salt would be liberally spread between each layer and the fish would be left to soak in this brine for several weeks. When they were suitably "pickled" they would be pitchforked out and taken across the road to the dryer building.

The dryer consisted of rows of stalls, each containing a dozen or so slide-out shelves made of a wooden frame covered with chicken wire. The fish would be laid out flat on these wire racks, the shelves pushed back in, the doors closed, and for the next several days a big fan at the end of the row would blow hot air from a furnace over them.

When the fish had reached the proper degree of dryness, they would be removed from the dryers and packed into wooden boxes, one hundred pounds of dried, salt-encrusted fish to a box. The lid would be nailed on, a wire strap bound around the box, and a black-ink stencil applied, identifying it as a Product of Canada, and its final destination, usually Jamaica, Barbados, the Dominican Republic or some other Caribbean country.

Back at the keeler, I could only dream of those warm, tropical islands. By the time our mid-morning break rolled around, after a couple hours of standing in several inches of ice-cold water and fish guts, I had to run home and soak my hands in warm water to get any feeling back. I had made the rookie mistake of working with bare hands instead of wearing gloves. In addition to the effect of the ice-cold sluice water, I also discovered that when you handle fish barehanded the scales would sometimes slide under your fingernails, which really hurt. I soon got used to working with gloves on.

## Two Ferries Out

I spent the next few summers at the fish plant. During that time I hoisted fish from the boats, drove the forklift, took truckloads of pickled fish to Joe Casey's fish business in Digby, built thousands of fish boxes, and loaded and emptied the dryers.

Two events remain most clearly in my mind from those years. The first one took place the second summer I worked in the plant. As was common in those days, waste from the plant was dropped through a hole in the floor directly into the water. It was mostly fish guts that went down the hole. Except for the liver, which was removed and saved in forty-five-gallon drums to be picked up by Gerald and Albert Baily for processing into fish oil. The backbone and head went out through a hole in the wall into a holding area known as the gurry bin. Every couple of days a little scow we called The Gurry Boat would arrive from Freeport to take away the odoriferous contents to be processed into fish meal.

One hot day in August, we realized that the scow hadn't been around for a while, and the bin was getting overly full. It turned out that the boat had broken down and would be out of commission for a while longer. A few days later, the bin was full to the point where the holes in the wall, where we threw the heads and bones out, were blocked, and a couple of us were elected to go into the bin and move things around to make more room.

The smell as we approached the bin was bad enough. Then, after a few seconds of slipping and sliding around, we noticed that our boots, shovels and the bottom of our barvels were covered with little wriggling creatures. The whole floor of the bin was a moving carpet of maggots! We quickly abandoned our assigned job and hosed down.

Fortunately, the next morning, the bin was empty: the Gurry Boat was back in action! I can't imagine what conditions on that boat were like after emptying half a dozen bins like ours.

The last year I worked at the plant, I witnessed an event that most likely will never be seen again. Early one evening, Albert Graham got his seine around a huge school of pollack just outside the harbour on the Bay of Fundy side. They needed help to handle this massive catch, and several boats went out to assist, arriving back loaded down with fish, every one of them fat and firm and at least three feet long.

Ray McDormand brought in a load, and when he started back out for the next one, I jumped aboard and went with him. We loaded up again, and when we headed back in, the boat was so full that the only place I could find to stand was on the washboard. We were so low in the water, I was afraid we would swamp before reaching the wharf. It looked like the wake behind the boat would wash right in over the stern if we slowed down too fast.

After the catch was totalled up, Dad's fishplant had its biggest day ever, over 106,000 pounds of fish brought in. Every part of the building was filled several feet deep—you had to walk on top of the fish to get around, ducking under the rafters as you went. The building was filled right to the front doors,

## Two Ferries Out

where fish were spilling out onto the side of the street.

Dad had to make an emergency run to Meteghan in his speedboat to get more workers. He set them up with a keeler and splitting table right on the side of the road. I remember some tourists walking by and asking what we were going to do with all those sharks!

**Ben Robicheau**

*Stopping for lunch on the way to Expo 67.*

## 19: The Robicheaus go to Expo 67

Of course, it wasn't all work and no play. 1967 was a year of national events and celebrations, it being Canada's one hundredth birthday; plus, it coincided with the holding of a World Exposition in Montreal. Like many other Canadian families, we discussed the possibility of going to Expo '67, but with news reports at the time talking about the shortage, and resulting high prices, of accommodations, our parents reluctantly decided that the cost of housing and feeding eleven people was just too much.

We kids had resigned ourselves to not getting to experience the bright lights of Montreal and the international excitement of Expo, when a visitor to the Island changed all that.

For years, every spring and fall, a travelling salesman from Montreal called on the Islands' stores. He always arrived in a late-model Cadillac, the trunk and back seat heaped high with his stock of dry goods.

While he was conducting business with our father, the subject of Expo came up, and Dad mentioned that he would like to go, but with nine kids, couldn't see how he could possibly afford it.

The salesman mentioned that he himself had been to Expo several times, and that it was a wonderful thing that all kids should get a chance to see. He also mentioned that he owned a cottage not too far from Montreal, and he could let us use it for free for a week. That night Dad announced that we were going to Expo after all.

A couple of weeks later, we were on our way! As if cramming two parents and nine kids, plus luggage, into one mid-sized station wagon wasn't enough, my sisters had convinced my parents that there was room for one more. A friend from Maine, Joyce Farnsworth, had just arrived to visit her grandmother for a few days, and the next thing she knew she was shoehorned into the back seat of our station wagon and on her way to Quebec.

These were the days before seat belt laws, so my sister Joyce and brother John, the two youngest, sat in the front seat between our parents, and the rest of the eight of us took turns sitting crammed on top of each other in the back seat, or lying uncomfortably way in the back, on top of the luggage.

When we finally arrived in Montreal, my father went to pick up the key to the cottage at an address the salesman had given him. It turned out to be Bens, a deli renowned in Quebec, indeed in all of Canada, for their smoked meat sandwiches. It seemed that the "travelling salesman" was in fact, the owner of several businesses, and owned not one, but two cottages side-by-side on a lake in the exclusive Laurentian Mountains.

My father returned to the car with the keys to both cottages and a huge deli tray of smoked meat

## Two Ferries Out

and cheese that had been presented to him. This served as our lunches for the next few days.

Expo was just as exciting as all the hype had made it seem. The impressive and distinctive geodesic dome of the U.S. pavilion, the British pavilion with its Union Jack-painted tower, Ontario with its high-tech, 360-degree slide and film show. The Nova Scotia pavilion featured a wooden schooner being built on site, and the Canada pavilion had its birthday theme song, which we heard everywhere ("CA-NA-DA, now we are 20 million"). Fair goers had 'passports' they could validate with a unique stamp at each pavilion. This made some of us want to visit countries based solely on how 'cool' their stamp was. At the end of each day, we would compare passport stamps.

La Ronde, the huge amusement park with the great rides, was even more impressive when it was all lit up at night. We even got to explore a bit of the city and ride on the recently-opened Montreal subway, unique at the time because it ran on rubber tires instead of rails.

After four days of visiting nearly every country in the world, getting lost, standing in line, feeling sick from too many hot dogs and too much sun, and still more standing in line, our time at Expo came to an end.

My father tended to have a heavy foot, and heading back to the cottage for our last night, he got stopped for speeding. The policeman told him he had to pay a fine, and because we were from out of province, it had to be paid on the spot. Dad informed him that he only had enough money for gas to get us home, and couldn't pay the fine. The policeman replied that there was no way out of it, either he paid the fine or he would go to jail.

Dad replied, "Okay, I guess you'll have to take me to jail, but that car has my wife and ten kids in it, none of them can drive." (Not true.) "You'll have to take them, too."

The policeman looked at the car, called his commanding officer, then, after a lot of back-and-forth on the police radio, told Dad that he guessed this time he'd make an exception and let him go with just a warning.

The next morning, we once again wedged ourselves into the car and began our two-day, pre-Trans-Canada-Highway trip home. All these years later, I still look back on this, the one and only trip we ever took as a complete family, as one of the highlights of my youth.

## 20: A trip to the New England states

The summer after our family trip to Expo, I got the opportunity to take another trip. In 1968, my brother-in-law, Don Bolstad, got a contract to tow five newly-built boats to Portsmouth, New Hampshire. Don was a salvage diver, and his boat was a heavy-duty work vessel, suitable for this type of work.

The boats he would be towing were Cape Island-style fishing boats built at the Meteghan River shipyard on the French Shore. Americans liked this type of boat, and also liked the fact that the exchange on the U.S. dollar at the time made it more economical for them to have their boats built in Canada. Since import duties were lower on unfinished hulls, four of the boats had no power; their engines would be installed once they got to the States. The fifth boat, which was a little fancier than the others and looked like it was intended more for pleasure than for work, was fully operational, outfitted with a V-8 engine that the owner had delivered while his boat was under construction.

Five boats are a lot to tow at one time, and could be too much for one person to handle safely, so Don asked if I would come along to help out. After picking up the boats, we towed them across St. Mary's Bay to Westport, where we prepared for the long tow to Portsmouth.

Thinking it would be a good idea to have a "back-up boat" in case of emergency, we decided to familiarize ourselves with the one operating boat by taking it out for a test run. Within minutes, we noticed that the engine temperature gauge had shot up into the danger zone. An investigation revealed that the cooling system had been hooked up incorrectly. After a bit of re-plumbing, another run around the harbour confirmed that we had corrected the problem.

That evening we headed out on an overnight crossing of the Bay of Fundy, with our tow bobbing along behind us like a row of oversized ducklings.

Dawn the next morning, found us following a southerly route among the picturesque islands off the Maine coast. We stopped at nightfall, and started out again at first light Friday morning. By noon, we had arrived at the mouth of the Piscataqua River, the border between Maine and New Hampshire.

Heading upriver to Portsmouth Harbor, we scanned the waterfront for an empty space big enough to dock six boats. The public wharf was crowded with a variety of fishing and pleasure craft, so no room there, but just upriver a bit we spotted an empty wharf. It looked a bit rundown, but had the room we needed, so would suit our purposes just fine.

## Two Ferries Out

After getting all of the boats safely tied up, we reported our arrival to the relevant authorities and then called the boat owners.

Late that afternoon, the first owner arrived to pay his share of the towing fee and pick up his new boat. On Saturday, two more were towed away, and the owner of another paid his fee and told us he would leave his boat where it was for a couple of days until he could arrange to have it towed.

The owner of the last boat, the one that could operate under its own power, had told us he would be there early Sunday morning. This was fine with us, as long as we could leave by noon. We wanted to be clear of the river and well on our way by nightfall.

Noon came and went with no sign of the owner. He finally arrived late in the afternoon, accompanied by a dozen boisterous friends and several cases of beer. He was in a big rush to get under way, because he lived a couple of hours down the coast and wanted to make it home before dark. After getting his entourage and his beer aboard, he started the engine and headed straight out without bothering to take a test run around the harbour or doing anything else to check the boat out. It was a good thing for him that we had discovered the cooling system problem back in Westport Harbour, or he and his beer-swigging pals would have had to deal with it somewhere off the coast of New Hampshire.

All the boats were now taken care of, and we still had just enough daylight left to safely get underway ourselves. We called Customs to tell them we were ready to leave, but by the time an agent came down to check us out and all the paperwork was done, it was getting too dark to navigate the unfamiliar waterway, so we decided to wait and leave at first light in the morning. We hit our bunks early, and settled in to get some sleep.

Some time around 1:30 in the morning, I awoke to the sound of the automatic bilge pump running. This was not an unusual sound; this pump started and stopped at random times as it pumped out any water that had accumulated in the bottom of the boat. But it had never woken me up before, what was different this time?

Don was still sound asleep in a lower bunk. It hadn't woken him, so maybe there was nothing to worry about. But then, Don was famous for being able to sleep through anything, a skill he picked up during his years in the Navy.

After a few minutes of lying there in the dark listening, I realized that the pump, which normally only needed to operate for a minute or two to pump out whatever water had accumulated, was running a lot longer than usual, so I decided to get up and investigate.

The water level in the bilge looked a bit higher than would be expected, and despite the stream that it was steadily shooting over the side, the pump didn't seem to be making much headway. To run the bigger auxiliary pump, I started up the engine, and saw the water level immediately start to drop. I went

## Two Ferries Out

back to my bunk for the couple of minutes it would take to pump out the boat.

Twenty minutes later, I awoke to the sound of the engine still running and Don shouting, "Get up! Get up! we're sinking!"

Jumping from my bunk, I landed in water nearly up to my knees. It flooded the cabin floor up to the level of Don's bunk, which is what had finally woken him. Rushing out on deck, we were both at a loss to understand what was happening. Where was the water coming from? Why were we sinking?

Don pulled out a hand-operated pump and yelled for me to go get the town fire department to bring one of their pumpers.

As I ran full-tilt for the fire-hall through the nearly deserted streets of late-night Portsmouth, two things occurred to me: number one: I was in my bare feet and had on no shirt, only a pair of jeans; and number two: I had absolutely no idea where the fire-hall was. Luckily, a couple of blocks from the waterfront, I came across a police station. A startled-looking Desk Sergeant seemed slightly confused as to why a half-naked person whose boat was sinking needed the Fire Department, but he informed me that it was another couple of blocks up the street, and two minutes later I was urgently punching their front door buzzer.

After what seemed like an eternity, a sleepy-eyed fireman appeared at the door and listened to my hastily explained request. As I completed my explanation for a second time, slower this time so he could understand what I required, the fire alarm went off.

The fireman said, "Sorry, gotta go. Call the Coast Guard", and slammed the door.

As I hot-footed it back to the police station, I cursed myself for not thinking of the obvious. The Coast Guard Station was half a mile away in Kittery; we had seen the white boats with the red slash coming and going right across the river from where we were docked.

Back at the police station, the Desk Sergeant was still confused about my problem, but called the Coast Guard for me. After they said they'd be right over, I high-tailed it back to the boat.

The situation had not improved in the short time I'd been gone. Don was still feverishly working the hand pump, but was now knee-deep in water. He had shut off the engine as the water rose around it, but the electric bilge pump was still going, still pumping water out of the side of the boat, except the port where the water came out, normally a foot or so above water, was now a few inches below water level. I told Don that the Coast Guard was on its way, grabbed a bucket and started bailing.

As Don and I bent to our tasks, we both strained to hear the Coast Guard cutter coming to our rescue. If we could just stay afloat long enough for them to get a pump aboard, we might be able to move our boat to shallow water somewhere and ground it out until we could figure out what was going on.

## Two Ferries Out

As the minutes ticked by, and our arms got progressively more tired, the water continued to rise. Finally, it became clear that our efforts were having no effect, the Coast Guard wasn't coming; we weren't going to be rescued. With only a couple of inches of freeboard showing, we abandoned ship.

As we sat on the wharf in the quiet darkness, listening to the soft bubbling and gurgling of the water, we finally heard the starting engines of the Coast Guard cutter echo from the other side of the river. Our hopes soared at the sound, only to be dashed as the water rose the final few millimetres over the side of our boat and it settled gently to the bottom of the harbour.

The Coast Guard arrived a couple of minutes later, to find only a few feet of mast and the top bit of cabin protruding from the water. They surveyed the scene and told us there was nothing they could do now; they'd be back in a few hours when the tide was down.

As the cutter disappeared into the night, we made our way over to the last remaining boat and climbed aboard. Just as we were settling in, trying to get comfortable on the cold, hard wood of the mattressless bunks, a shout came from the wharf. A town cop had noticed our situation, and was checking to see if everyone was alright.

We stepped out of the cabin to assure him we were okay. Seeing the two of us in nothing but wet jeans, he suggested it might be a good idea if we came up to the Station to warm up and dry out. So, for the third time that night, I made my way to the Portsmouth Police Station.

At the station, the Desk Sergeant rummaged among some used clothing kept on hand for their less fortunate visitors—which now, I guess, included us—and came up with a couple of shirts and a selection of shoes for us to try on. I found a nice pair of penny loafers that fit okay; Don, with his size-thirteen feet, had a little more trouble, and had to settle for a pair of dressy black wingtips.

Once we were outfitted, we were led down a corridor and shown our room for the night: the drunk tank! We were relieved to find it had been a quiet Sunday night and we were the only guests.

We stretched out on the bare, plastic-covered bunks, trying hard to ignore the glare of the always-on hundred-watt light bulb in the middle of the ceiling, and made an attempt to get some shut-eye. Just before I dozed off, I heard Don say, "What the Hell happened? Please tell me this is all just a bad dream."

I woke up the next morning in a condition probably familiar to most people who have had the misfortune to spend the night in a drunk tank: feeling tired, rough, and clinging to the faint hope that the events that had brought us here had been nothing more than a nightmare. But the truth all too quickly came rushing back: Don and I had indeed spent the night as guests of the Portsmouth Police Department.

## Two Ferries Out

I worried for a few seconds that whoever was now on duty would think that we were a couple of vagrants or winos, instead of unfortunate victims of circumstance who needed a warm place to spend the night. I was relieved to see that the cell door was still open, and that we were able to walk out without setting off any alarms. After thanking our hosts for the accommodations, we headed for the waterfront in our unfashionable shirts and borrowed shoes just as the sun was rising.

Back at the wharf, our predicament was starting to attract some attention. The tide was now falling and more of the boat was above water; as daylight increased and waterfront workers arrived, a crowd started to gather. People from neighbouring boats began showing up with various items they had found floating around the dock, and we were soon offered help from all quarters.

We still had no idea what had caused this disaster. Don wanted to get in the water and check out the bottom of the boat, but all his diving gear was still aboard and was now unusable, covered in a foul mixture of diesel fuel and engine oil.

A member of the crowd said he had gear we could use, and was back in minutes with a complete SCUBA outfit.

After making a survey of the hull, Don reported that there appeared to be several broken planks, and that the harbour floor right under the boat seemed to be covered with pointed posts. This caused one of the observers to recall that about a year or two previously, the city had started to tear down the wharf, then abruptly abandoned the job. A building had been removed, and a crane had pulled out the posts it stood on. Some of them had broken off a foot or two above the harbour floor and the stumps had been left sticking up out of the mud. We had tied up above these posts.

Luckily, on our first two nights, the tide didn't go down quite low enough for us to make contact with the jagged post remainders, but last night's tide was the lowest of the month, dropping just far enough to set us down on them. Don used his boat mainly for diving and salvage work. The deck was covered with protective steel plates; and it had a heavy-duty winch with several hundred feet of steel cable, a steel mast and boom, and a big diesel engine. All this extra weight sitting on these posts had cracked some of the planks and, as the tide rose again, the boat filled with water.

Now we knew what had caused our problem, but what could we do about it? Don went back in the water to saw off the post tops and patch the most obvious holes.

By now, the tide was all the way down, and the Coast Guard had returned. They put a gas-powered pump aboard, and within minutes we were floating freely again.

Their plan was to tow us across to the Maine side of the river, where there were two shipyards. One was the Portsmouth Naval Yard, where the first U.S. Navy submarine was built in 1917, and the first

## Two Ferries Out

American nuclear sub was launched in 1957; our destination was a commercial shipyard right next door to the Navy yard.

As we headed across the harbour, it quickly became apparent that Don's patch job had been incomplete. Water was coming in at a rate that the pump could just barely keep up with. Halfway across, the pump began to sputter; we were able to keep it going, but at a slower speed, and now the water began to gain on us. By the time we neared the Maine side, we were once again settling low and the floorboards were awash. Then the pump quit altogether.

To get boats out of the water, the shipyard had a large cradle that they rolled down an incline. You tied your boat in position over it, and they then hauled you up into the yard. Our problem right now was that we might be too deep in the water to be able to get in over the cradle. We were sinking lower by the second, and in serious danger of foundering in deep water only a few yards from safety.

After some frantic manoeuvring, we managed to scrape our keel over the cradle bar, get into position and then, for the second time that day, sink to the bottom. Except this time, we settled safely onto the cradle.

With the boat out of the water, we were now able to assess the damage. The interior of the boat and all its contents, including all our clothes and personal items, were covered in an oily slime. The engine needed to be taken apart and all its parts flushed and assessed for damage, and the batteries and electrical system tested and replaced if necessary. Taking a good look at the bottom of the boat, we saw that there were more broken and cracked planks than we had first realized.

Dwayne, the yard's head carpenter, recommended replacing all the damaged planks, but Don said he couldn't afford that. He'd just cover the holes with plywood patches and have the permanent repairs done back in Nova Scotia.

Upon hearing where we were from, Dwayne asked if we happened to know a place called Brier Island, and a fellow by the name of Raymond Robicheau. It turned out that for many years Dwayne and his friend James had spent their summer vacations sailing up and down the coast, and on one of these trips, had run into engine trouble crossing the Bay of Fundy. They made it to Westport, where my father had helped them out by letting them make phone calls to find the required engine parts and then lending his truck so they could go pick up those parts.

Now, it was Dwayne's turn to repay the favour. He said Don's plywood plan was not safe, and that there was no way he would let us leave with patches on the hull, he'd do a proper job and replace the planks himself, at no charge.

He also arranged free accommodations for us. The yard owner had built a cozy little apartment on a barge he owned, when his wife had kicked him out of the house the previous summer. Luckily for us, she had recently taken him back and the barge apartment was now vacant.

## Two Ferries Out

With our basic shelter taken care of, we got to work on the boat. First, we stripped out everything that was removable. All the clothes and bedding went to the laundromat, where hot water and copious amounts of detergent took out most of the oil. Then we steam-cleaned the interior and left all the doors, windows and hatches open to dry things out.

When the engine was disassembled, we found that the head had warped when it submerged into cold water while still hot. On his own time, the yard owner drove the head seventy miles to a shop that could grind it flat again, waited several hours for the work to be done, then delivered it back to us: no charge.

Dwayne's sailing buddy, James, worked at the Navy Yard next door, and he snuck our two heavy-duty batteries in to be drained, flushed and recharged. He also managed to conveniently find some "surplus" electrical cable to replace our battery straps that the reaction of electricity to salt water had corroded away.

While all this was going on, Dwayne was working away at repairing the damage to the hull. Because he could only work on it in his spare time, it was going rather slowly. This was partly because it was a time-consuming job. The damaged planks had to be chiselled out and removed, new ones cut and fitted, seams caulked and the new wood painted. But it was also going slow because Dwayne suffered from narcolepsy: if he relaxed for more than a few seconds, he would fall asleep. After twice discovering him sitting under the boat, fast asleep with his hammer and chisel in his hands, I started to keep an eye on him. If he dozed off, I would hammer on the hull to wake him up.

After five hectic days of cleaning up, drying out, taking things apart and putting them back together again, we were finally ready to head home. At the last minute, we discovered that the alternator wasn't working. This meant our batteries weren't charging, so if we shut the engine off, we might not be able to start it again.

Don came up with a simple, yet practical, solution: we just wouldn't shut off the engine until we got home!

We tentatively made our way north, at first, not straying too far from the coast in case any undiscovered problems arose. By the time we started across the Bay of Fundy from Grand Manan Island, we were feeling pretty confident in our repair work, and arrived safely back in Westport with no further mishaps.

Even though we weren't overly thrilled about the reason for our extended stay, the people we met in Maine and New Hampshire were terrific! They treated us to meals, invited us into their homes, worked for free, gave us supplies and equipment, drove us places; in short, did everything that they possibly could to help us out.

The U.S. Government wasn't quite so hospitable, however. About a month after we arrived home, Don got a letter informing him that he was being charged

## Two Ferries Out

with leaving the country without clearing customs, and we would have to pay a fine of twelve hundred dollars. He replied that we *had* cleared customs, but our departure was delayed due to an improperly-demolished wharf. This, plus the fact that there were no warning signs on the wharf, and no mention of the poor condition of the wharf from the several Government officials who had visited us, seemed like it might provide a good basis for a suit for damages.

A few weeks later, a letter arrived advising him that the charges had been dropped, and the fine cancelled.

**Ben Robicheau**

*Annie's Barn.*

## 21: A woman ahead of her time

Like any community, Brier Island had its collection of what we might call odd ducks. Those people who were slightly eccentric, differently thinking, or somehow not quite in sync with the majority. For the most part, as long as they did not bother anyone else, the community overlooked and accepted their oddities. Looking back from the perspective of the present day, some of those people who we looked on as being slightly outside the norm were in fact, exemplifying attributes that we now tend to admire and encourage.

Annie Moore was one such person.

Whenever anyone spoke of Annie Moore, they almost always used her full name. I rarely heard anyone call her Mrs. Moore, or just Annie, unless they were talking to her. If they were talking *about* her, it was always 'Annie Moore'. I'm not sure why this was, because, as far as I can remember, she was the only Annie on the Island, so there was no danger of being unclear as to who it was you were talking about.

Besides, the community had a well-established system in place for avoiding identity problems. If two women had the same first name, at least one of them would have her name spliced to her husband's first name. This was the case with Alma-Wally, who lived on the back road beside the new school; and of course, there was also Edna-Fred, who lived right across the lane from Edna Bowers, so it was pretty obvious where confusion could arise there. For some reason, this double-name solution only applied to women, if two men had the same name, one of them got a nickname, like Lawrence 'Brooks' Gower, Arnold 'Duffy' Titus, or Bernard 'Ace' McDormand.

It may be that people thought Annie required a bigger name because she had a bigger personality than most people. I remember her as being a tallish, raw-boned kind of woman, with a booming voice, and a face and hands that always looked red and weathered. She usually wore a long tweed coat and sturdy walking shoes, or rubber boots, depending on how muddy the road between town and Northern Light was that day.

For some reason, part of her regular routine was to pay a visit to my mother on Mondays, which was laundry day. I can still see her in our kitchen, sitting against the wall on a straight-backed wooden kitchen chair amid the steam and soapsuds from the washtubs of wet clothes that took up the majority of floor space, the wringer washer churning away in the background. Even in the heat of the kitchen, she'd usually be all bundled up in her hat and buttoned-up coat, chatting away at my mother as she tried to do the laundry, get supper ready, and keep track of several kids, always one or more of them in diapers. And when Annie chatted, you paid attention! She talked in a very loud voice, possibly the result of living next door to a foghorn for a good part of her life.

For many years, Annie and her husband, Fred, were the keepers of Northern Light. The last few years they lived there, Fred suffered from a long and debilitating illness. After he got too sick to drive, Annie would walk two and a half miles from Northern Point every week to my father's store across from the ferry wharf, to do her grocery shopping. Occasionally, if the weather was bad, or she had an extra-large order, she would accept a ride home, or have her groceries delivered, but for the most part, she would have her supplies packed into a cardboard box tied up with twine, and then carry them home herself.

She was always very particular about the box. It had to be sturdy, with the top flaps still attached; the boxes that Carnation Milk came in were perfect for the job, being strong and just the right size. My father usually cut the tops off of the boxes when unpacking the freight, but would keep a few good boxes with the flaps intact just for Annie. The twine had to be strong, also, because that's what she used to carry the box; it must have been hard on the fingers toting a box full of groceries back up the hill to the High Knoll and along the dirt road back home to Northern Light.

Annie did all this walking even though she and Fred had a car, a Hudson Super Six from the early 40s. It was Fred's pride and joy. He kept it in great shape, and after he passed away several people offered to buy it. Annie wouldn't sell and kept it stored away in the garage; she had never learned to drive despite living at an isolated end of the Island a couple of miles from her nearest neighbour.

A couple of years after Fred died, she had the car driven to a field across from Daniel Kenney's barn where it was left, abandoned to the elements. The car slowly deteriorated over the years, and eventually was bulldozed into the ground, I guess she couldn't stand to see anyone else driving her husband's baby.

Eventually Annie moved from Northern Point, I don't know if it was her own decision, or if the Government forced her out. It's possible that they thought a woman couldn't operate a lighthouse on her own, even though Annie had been doing just that for all the years that Fred had been bedridden, and for a few more years after his death. In any case, she made the move into town, but just barely. She bought the last house on the very edge of the village, the one closest to Northern Point.

My father had offered to help her move, and when he arrived at the lightkeeper's house, he was surprised to see all of those Carnation boxes again. She had hundreds of them, all neatly tied up with the carrying string, mostly filled with what looked to be empty tin cans and glass bottles and jars. My father said that for every truckload of furniture he hauled, he hauled three more of boxes. I don't think anyone knows for sure why she had been saving all this stuff for so long. Dad thinks that maybe she got into the habit during the Second World War, when everybody saved everything to be recycled for the War Effort, and she just never gave it up. Whatever the reason, by the time she was moved into her new home, a good part of it was taken up with her boxes.

Annie rarely let anyone into her house, I occasionally delivered groceries to her, and was always instructed to leave them outside the back door. I did get inside on one occasion, several years after she moved in. She was having trouble with her kitchen stove and asked me in to take a look at it. It appeared to me that she was living in just two rooms, the crowded kitchen seemed to be her main living area, and I could see that what had been the dining room now had a bed in it. The former living room looked to be mostly full of boxes and stacks of old newspapers, and I assume the other five or six rooms in the big old house must have been in a similar condition.

It wasn't just tin and glass that Annie stockpiled. She also scoured the beach for driftwood that she then hauled home and cut up for firewood. It wasn't an unusual sight to see her, well into her 70s by now, wrestling a four-foot stick of water-soaked pulpwood up over the breastwork. Many people won't burn driftwood; it's usually wet and saturated with salt, which will eventually rust out the bottom of your stove. But Annie had worked out a system to minimize this problem. She piled the newly salvaged wood in her back yard for a year or so to let the rain and snow wash away most of the surface salt. Then she cut and split it, and left it stacked outside for another year; then she finally moved it into an old barn she had on the property. By the time she was ready to burn it, the wood was well dried and mostly salt-free.

Over the years, her woodpile grew and grew, far beyond what she could possibly use in a lifetime, the small barn was eventually filled to the rafters. In fact, it was so full that I think it was only the wood stacked inside that kept the decrepit old structure from falling down. When the building wouldn't hold any more, she stacked the wood in the yard in neat circular piles.

The last few years she lived in the house, I'm not sure she even burned wood anymore, I know that at some point she had an oil stove installed in the kitchen. But she kept on gathering wood off the beach and piling it up in her yard. I think that, like the cans and bottles, collecting driftwood was a habit she found impossible to break; she just couldn't bear to see all that potential firewood go to waste.

How Annie Moore chose to live her life may have caused some people to categorize her as eccentric or compulsive, but, as is the case in many small communities, the people of Brier Island knew her for the whole person she was. They knew there was more to her than her sometimes-unusual behaviour, they accepted her for who she was, and left her alone to live her life as she saw fit.

In fact, she could be considered as a woman ahead of the times. She lived a good part of her life as an independent woman, relying on her own resources and efforts to support herself in the way that she wanted, living life on her own terms. And long before anyone else started talking about saving the environment by reducing, recycling and reusing, Annie Moore was already doing it.

**Ben Robicheau**

## 22: Ace – trial by fire

One of the aspects of living in any small town is that you get to know your neighbours extremely well. This is even more so on an island, where everyone is restricted to the same geographic area.

In the fifties and sixties, the relative remoteness of our particular location made intrusion or assistance from the outside world even more rare than it is today. As a result, of necessity, Brier Islanders were, and still are, fiercely independent and at the same time, almost entirely reliant on each other for help in times of emergency.

As a child, it did not seem unusual to me that I would know everyone in my community and that everyone knew me. Every person in town played some part in my growing up; but all these years later, there are a few who tend to shine a bit brighter in my memory. This story is mostly from the long-ago perspective of a young person. As far as I know, or can recall, this is what happened. It may or may not be entirely accurate.

"Ace" McDormand got his nickname because, when he was a young man, he and his brothers had an obsession with playing card games. He was so well-known by this name that few people knew his real one. One day, a man from the Fisheries Dept. arrived looking for Bernard McDormand. Several people told him, quite definitely, that there was no one of that name on the Island. Finally, he tried the store by the ferry wharf, where the men on the bench all said he must be mistaken, there was no Bernard McDormand that they knew of. Probably thinking that he somehow had arrived at the wrong island, or that there was some conspiracy to keep him in the dark, the man was about to leave when the storekeeper, Gladys Bailey, spoke up. Gladys prided herself on knowing everything about everybody, and she was more than happy to inform the visitor, as well as the crew on the bench, that Bernard was in fact, Ace's real name.

Ace possessed a self-taught talent for fixing the old car engines that powered most of the local fishing boats. His unique methods being somewhat free and easy, he often ended up with a few bits and pieces left over after completing the job. His philosophy was, "If it runs without those parts, it doesn't really need them anyway."

One year, a few days before lobster season, he spent hours tied up at the wharf, tinkering with his engine, trying to get it running properly. Finally, in a fit of exasperation at his lack of success, he hoisted the engine out of the boat, swung it over the side, and dropped it into twenty feet of water. The next morning, it dawned on him that the season opened in a couple of days, and he didn't have power for his boat. At low tide, he went down on the beach, hoisted the engine back in the boat, and a couple of days later had it running well enough to go fishing.

## Two Ferries Out

It could be said of Ace that, in some respects, "If he didn't have bad luck, he'd have no luck at all." Most of Ace's bad luck involved fire and water, usually at the same time.

We were half-way through Sunday School lessons one sunny summer morning when a long plume of black smoke drifting over the harbour distracted us from the minister's sermon. Sunday School was abruptly cancelled, and we all rushed outside where we could see that the oily cloud appeared to be coming from "up the road".

The source of the smoke turned out to be Ace's boat. I arrived on the scene to see it lying on its side, half-sunk in shallow water on the beach beside his wharf. Donald, Ace's teenaged son, sat on the wharf, obviously upset and in pain from a singed face and hand.

The story emerged that Donald had rowed out to the moorings to bring the boat in to the wharf to unload some fish caught the day before. It was a hot, sunny day, and a can of gas stored in the cabin had filled the boat with fumes. This being Ace's boat, he had "temporarily" solved some electrical problem he was having by putting his battery in the cabin and rigging it up with jumper cables leading to the engine. When Donald hit the starter button, the haphazard electronics created a spark which ignited the gas fumes, shooting a ball of fire out the open cuddy door and into the wheelhouse where Donald was standing, burning him and setting the boat ablaze.

**Ben Robicheau**

Donald, frightened and in pain, jumped back in the punt and headed for shore. Ace and some of his neighbours went out to the moorings and towed the burning boat into shallow water, where they sank her by chopping a hole below the waterline, putting the fire out and saving what was left of the boat.

The next episode in Ace's fire-related trilogy happened on a Sunday as well. I remember lying in bed well past the usual time, and wondering why I wasn't being called to get ready for Sunday School. When I eventually went downstairs, I found two piles of smelly, wet clothes in the middle of the kitchen floor. By now the rest of the kids were up and we went to our parents' room to find out what was going on. There, we found them still in bed and obviously exhausted.

Dad looked at us, and said, "Ace's house burned down last night."

Ace had awoken sometime after midnight to find his house full of smoke. At the time, there was no organized fire department to call, so Ace and Donald started carrying furniture out of the house while his wife Arlene alerted the next-door neighbour. A phone call was made to Elsie the switchboard operator, who rang people all over the Island. When Dad got the call, he immediately went to his store, where he gathered up all the buckets he could find. Meanwhile, a group of men headed to the old barn where the "fire pump" was kept.

The fire pump was a trailer with a large pump mounted on it. The town had purchased this rig, along with hoses and some other basic equipment, several years earlier, after a previous fire. Unfortunately, no arrangements had been made for regular practice with, or maintenance of, the equipment. An old car engine, which hadn't been started in quite some time, supplied power for the pump.

By the time they managed to get the trailer hooked up and towed to the scene of the fire, a bucket brigade was already at work. A line of men and women was transporting water up from the beach in a futile attempt to keep the fire under control. Hoses were rolled out and the key was turned to start the engine. Nothing; the battery was dead. Quickly, a battery was pulled from someone's truck, and now the engine turned over, but still wouldn't start.

While the men worked feverishly to get the pump going, the fire continued to grow, and the by-now-exhausted bucket brigade continued to toss water at it. Finally, to everyone's relief, the engine coughed and finally sputtered to life.

As the pump started to pump, some men grabbed the hoses, ready to douse the now raging inferno. Noticing a lack of water pressure, they found that the old hoses had split under the strain. They switched out the hoses again and again, until some were found that could stand the pressure. Meanwhile, the engine kept stalling and the fire kept growing until, in the end, Aces' house burned to the ground.

But the fire pump was instrumental in saving the Garrons' house on one side and the Thompsons' on the other from suffering more than minor damage. And this incident inspired the town to organize the volunteer fire department that exists today.

Aces' second boat-related incident took place a few years later. I was rummaging around in the back porch of our house when I heard what I thought was a rumble of thunder. After a minute or two, it dawned on me that there was not a cloud in the sky, so it couldn't be thunder.

I ran outside to see, once again, a thick cloud of black smoke rising above the harbour.

I took off on my bike, heading down the road towards the ferry wharf. There stood Ace on the wharf at Dan Kenney's fish plant, and there, between Kenney's and the breakwater, amid a litter of wreckage, lay what was left of his boat, blasted apart, adrift and on fire, its cabin and deck gone and its stern board blown out.

As I watched, a fishing boat hooked a line to the burning shell and towed it away from the wharves and other boats and out into the open harbour where it could harmlessly burn itself out.

Again, the disaster had involved gasoline. While fuelling up at Kenney's wharf, Ace had wedged the nozzle open and left it running in the old oil drum that served as a gas tank, and then gone below. This was not an uncommon practice. It took some time to fill a forty-five-gallon drum and fishermen usually had other things to keep them busy while the drum was filling. But Ace apparently lost track of time and only remembered the nozzle when he became aware of the overpowering smell of gasoline. He emerged from the cabin to see a fine spray of gas spurting into the air from the over-filled tank, pouring onto the deck and down into the bilge.

Ace had left his engine running, and quickly realized that he had only seconds before the fumes from the gas met with an electrical spark or hot exhaust pipe. He made a leap for the wharf ladder and was about halfway up when a terrific explosion boosted him the final few feet onto the wharf.

Not one to be easily defeated, Ace had the burned and blasted hull of the boat towed back ashore, and then up into his front yard. There he went to work, replacing the deck and cabin, putting in a new stern board, and re-caulking the boat all over.

The interior of the hull was black and charred, and the whole boat needed a coat of paint. Luckily, Ace had recently been to a Government surplus auction, where he had been the successful bidder on several five-gallon cans of paint. This now came in handy, and the boat soon had a new paint job, in fact, at one point, his boat, house and car were all painted the same shade of Government Orange.

Within a few weeks, Ace was back on the water, going fishing miles offshore in all kinds of weather in that same boat. Unfortunately, despite his continuous caulking and patching, the boat always leaked like a sieve after the big explosion, and Ace had to be constantly pumping her out. If he was going to be away for a few days, he would bring the boat in to his wharf and tie it as far up the beach as possible, where if it was going to fill and sink, it would only drop a few inches until it was safely sitting high and (mostly) dry on the beach.

Ace lived a basic and humble life, with a few dramatic turns that some might say would make a good movie, which would be appropriate since Ace had a surprising connection to the bright lights and glamour of Hollywood as the uncle of acclaimed actress Frances McDormand.

It took stamina, resilience, strength, and self-reliance to survive as a fisherman on Brier Island in those days. Ace was the ultimate example of that. He took some hard knocks in his life, including one that many of us would find hard to bear, the loss of his son Donald at sea. Somehow, he was able to survive all that life threw at him, and lived to a ripe old age. He was one of the last of the old-style fishermen of Brier Island.

## 23: Iron Will

It's a warm August day in Westport. One of those rare summer days where you glance up from whatever you're doing and have to squint your eyes against the unexpectedly brilliant, crystal-clear glare of the sun sparking off the ripples in the harbour. In the Cove, across the harbour on the Freeport side, you can easily make out the distinct shapes and colours of the boats at their moorings. Then, a short while later, you look up again, and the end of the wharf and everything beyond it, has disappeared into a thick, grey nothingness!

This happens regularly on sunny summer Island days, the fog drifting continuously in and out of the passage. Thick as mud one minute, clear as crystal the next. But never completely gone, always seeming to hang just offshore, menacingly close to the Island. Close enough that it keeps the foghorns droning all day, regardless of whether the harbour is filled with nothing denser than sun and fresh air, or socked in under a pea-soup pall.

At the present moment, the fog is in, and I'm standing on the end of my father's wharf peering out into what my grandfather Terence used to call, "A t'ick o' fog." I can hear the ka-chunk-thunk, ka-chunk-thunk, ka-chunk-thunk sound clear enough, but I can't quite tell which direction the familiar sound is coming from. I'm straining my eyes to see through the pea soup. Fog reflects and distorts sound, so my ears aren't much help in determining from which direction the continuous ka-chunk-thunk is coming. The sound is steadily drawing closer, and I'm just zeroing in on a likely section of the fog wall, when the bow of a small craft materializes through the mist, just a few feet to the right of where I'm looking. Slowly, a weather-faded and well-worn red rowboat slips out from behind the curtain of fog. Steadily pulling on the oars, which are ka-chunk-thunking back and forth between the wooden thole pins with each stroke, is a short, burly gnome of a man with a round, ruddy face and a large drooping moustache.

As I expected, Will Thurber has arrived to sell today's meagre catch.

Will Thurber had been a fisherman for pretty much all of his life. Eventually, after sixty years on the sea, he decided that he had reached that point in his life where he could sell his boat, retire and do what he enjoyed most, which was...well...fishing! With only his rowboat now, and the bare minimum of gear, his expenses were low, so if the weather was bad, or the tide was wrong, or he just didn't feel up to it today, he could afford to stay in and miss a day's fishing.

Still, the days he did miss were few and far between. On almost any day of the week, from early spring to late fall, you could see Will's little boat in the harbour. He did pretty much all his fishing inside the harbour now, mostly around Peter's Island, ven-

## Two Ferries Out

turing just outside the passage only occasionally, when the weather and the tide were right. He liked to tie his bow-line to the marker buoy out in the middle of the harbour, and that was most often where you would see him, floating over the ledge that ran between the buoy and Peter's Island.

Judging by the grooves cut into the gunnels, Will must have spent many an hour sawing away on a handline over the side of his little rowboat. I'm sure he didn't begrudge a single minute of the time he used up trying to entice a decent-sized pollock or the occasional codfish out from the safety of the ledge, but the truth is that the harbour is not the most productive fishing ground. But then, I don't think Will really cared how much he caught. He'd had his day of fishing for a living; what he was doing now was something different.

Still, an important part of the process was selling up at the end of the day. The size of his catch may not have mattered all that much to Will, but it did to the people he tried to sell it to.

At first, Will sold to the fishplant closest to where he moored his boat, the one on Fish Point. Unfortunately, this Freeport plant was in the process of transitioning to catering to seiners and draggers, big boats bringing in thousands of pounds at a time. Will, in his little rowboat with his dozen or so fish, was just not worth bothering with.

He couldn't believe it when they eventually told him they weren't interested in dealing with him anymore. After all, his fish were just as good as anyone else's; better than some, in fact. Sure, he might not have a lot, and maybe some were a bit on the small side, but his fish were top quality, fresh and handled with care, caught just minutes away, not like the crushed and mangled, days-old stuff from miles offshore that was being hauled out of the holds of those draggers.

Rejected from the only fishplant in Freeport, Will crossed the passage to sell on the Westport side. Sadly, he didn't fare much better across the harbour. After a few weeks at the first plant, they came to the conclusion that it wasn't worth the effort to roll the cart down the ramp for his few fish, and asked Will to move along.

He gradually worked his way along the waterfront, spending time at each fish buyer before being forced along to the next. Finally, he came to the last buyer on the Westport waterfront: my father.

To my father's credit, he recognized that selling his fish was not about the money for Will. Being able to sell his catch gave Will a justification for doing what he loved to do. Dad decided that as long as Will was able to catch fish, he would buy them, no matter how few and far between they might be.

Which is how I came to be standing on the end of the wharf staring into the fog. It was my job to lower the bucket so Will could happily pitch in his day's catch, usually pausing to proudly hold up a particularly nice specimen for my admiration. Then I would hoist the fish, weigh them, and dump them into a chute to transport them to the main building for processing. When the last fish had been dealt with, I would lower the empty bucket with a paper slip attached, his receipt, detailing how many pounds of each type of fish Will had delivered. He could take this slip to my father's store to 'settle up', either in cash or in trade.

Our transaction completed, Will would again take to his oars and head home across the Passage; or if a Freeport boat happened to arrive at the wharf, he would patiently wait until they were done, then toss them his bow line and get towed home. He also used this method with the ferry. If the tide was against him and it looked like a tough row home, he would just make a short jog down to the ferry slip.

Eventually, Will acquired an outboard motor, an antiquated machine that was quite temperamental and often wouldn't start, so he still had to do some rowing now and then, but was able to get a break from the oars on the intermittent occasions when his motor actually worked.

My mother used to worry about Will. She thought it was dangerous for a man of his advanced years to be out in such a small boat. The weather could turn bad, and there was a risk of getting lost or run down in the fog. He must have been eighty or more by now; and in fact, on a couple of occasions, when the tide had been too strong for him to row against, the Coast Guard had had to rescue him after he was swept out through the passage into St. Mary's Bay.

But Will was doing what he enjoyed, what he had always done, and he had a life-time of experience with the sea to fall back on. Then, one day it seemed that my mother's worst fears had come to pass.

Our house was just across the road from the fish-plant. I was sitting at the kitchen table eating lunch when Mom yelled from the front room for me to run down to the wharf right away.

As I dashed out the door, I saw what my mother had seen from the front window, a little red rowboat floating beside our wharf with what appeared to be a motionless body face-down over the back, the head dangling over the stern board and both arms hanging in the water.

As I got closer to the scene and still saw no movement, I started to think maybe Will had finally suffered a heart attack or something, and was just wondering what I was going to do about that, when suddenly the body in question arose, and sat up with a piece of fishing line in his hand. While waiting for someone to come hoist his fish, Will had decided to put the time to good use by freeing a line that had got tangled in his propeller.

My mother continued to worry for another couple of years, until there finally came a spring when the little red rowboat failed to appear in the harbour. Eighty years of venturing out on the water in every season and in every kind of weather; eighty years of frostbite and sunburn and swollen, red, salt-water-stinging, rope-burned hands; eighty years of seeing spectacular sunsets rise and sink below the distant horizon; eighty years of reading the wind and the tide and watching whales at play had come to an end. Will Thurber had finally retired from the sea.

**Ben Robicheau**

*Elsie at the switchboard.*

## 24: Hello, Elsie

Today's technology makes it possible for people to be connected in more ways than ever before. It is not uncommon for people to have a personal cell phone, home land-line phone, work cell, and office phone; plus a home e-mail address, work e-mail, and maybe a G-mail address or two 'just in case'. People can also communicate through Facebook, Twitter, or a dozen other social media forums. And of course, as a last resort, there's what many people now consider the old-fashioned way: sit down and put pen to paper, put the letter in an envelope, and stick it in the mail; snail mail some call it.

Today, people have become so accustomed to near-constant contact that we take it for granted without really appreciating it. This was brought home to us personally in 2004 when our daughter volunteered for an infrastructure rebuilding project in rural Costa Rica. In order to talk to us in those days before cell phones were common everywhere, Sarah had to fend off the occasional wild dog pack while hiking for an hour on trails and dirt roads to get to the nearest town, where she then had to stand in line for a chance to use the only public phone in the only store in the village. Once she got to the phone, it was usually hit-and-miss on whether the long-distance system was functioning and would allow her to make an international call, and if she successfully passed that hurdle and got through to our number, we might not be home to accept her call.

After several missed calls, we began to make sure at least one of us was home all the time. When she did get us, she often felt a bit restricted in what she could say because everyone in the store was able to overhear her conversation; also, her time was limited because the next person in line was standing right behind her waiting for their turn to make a call.

A couple of years later, Sarah went to work in the Philippines for the summer. This time, she was provided all the modern conveniences. She was working in an office, in a city, and was supplied with a cell phone and Internet access. The phone didn't work all that well for international calls, so she ended up using it mostly for texting. For calls, we installed Skype on our computer and this worked great. It felt very futuristic to be able to call someone part-way around the world and see them as you talked with them.

It was not all that long ago when just being able to hear another person's voice over a wire seemed like an incredible thing. The first phone that I can remember was a big wooden box that hung on the wall in our Brier Island home. For some reason, this modern convenience had been installed in our unheated porch, so you had to almost go outside to use the phone, not too comfortable in the winter. It made for very brief conversations.

## Two Ferries Out

The wooden box was made of some kind of varnished hardwood, possibly oak, and had a little shelf on the front. An adjustable arm stuck out just above this shelf and held the mouthpiece, a black Bakelite cup that you spoke into. On the right side of the box was another cup connected to a wire; you held this up to your ear in order to hear the person on the other end. On the left side of the box was a little crank. To call someone on your line you just turned this crank to produce a series of long and short rings. Each phone customer on the line had a set of distinctive rings, one long and three short or two short and one long, or some variation of this pattern.

A couple of the fancier people on the Island had their own private lines, but this was more expensive, so most of us made do with the party line. Several people shared each party line, so when someone called, it would ring in every house on that line, and everyone would know by the series of rings who the call was for. If you wanted to make a call, you would have to first pick up the earpiece and listen, to make sure no one else was using the line. Sometimes you might have to ask some long-winded neighbour to get off the line so you could use it.

Every party line seemed to have at least one person who couldn't resist the urge to listen in on other people's calls. Anyone talking on a party line would be wise to assume that there might be a silent third party listening in, and occasionally would have their suspicions confirmed when the listener would forget they weren't supposed to be there, and spontaneously joined the conversation.

Despite its limitations, there were times when being on a party line came in handy. If you were next door, and someone rang your number, you could answer from your neighbour's house; or if you were expecting a call but were not going to be at home, you could ask someone else on the same line to pick up and take a message if they heard your number being called. Once in a while, some important event would take place that affected the whole community, and when the phone rang, everybody on the line might pick up, no matter who it was for.

If you wanted to call someone who wasn't on your own party line, you had to go through the operator. For many years, the switchboard for the Islands was located in Freeport at the home of Elsie Young. Elsie's job was not an easy one. She was basically on duty twenty-four hours a day, seven days a week; although once in a while, a caller would be momentarily startled to be greeted by the gruff voice of her husband Charlie on the line, giving Elsie a break. Several of the Island's teen-age girls also worked part-time over the years as relief operators, so the Youngs could have some time away from the maze of plugs and wires.

The phone number you gave the operator consisted of the line the person was on, and then their number on that line; written down it might look like 22-4, which translated to "twenty-two ring four" when you spoke it.

In addition to connecting the caller with the correct customer, Elsie was often called upon to take or pass along messages, look up phone numbers and act as our own emergency operator. In those pre-911 days, if some disaster happened on the Islands, all you had to do was call Elsie and let her know about it, and she would handle it from there by alerting the appropriate people.

If anyone wanted reliable information as to what was happening on either island, Elsie could most likely fill them in. Due to her position, she must have inadvertently come across a lot of juicy gossip, but as far as I know, she was very good at keeping it to herself.

In some ways, Elsie was almost a wizard at her job, often knowing who it was you wanted to call even before you told her. I remember my father, who had a habit of blanking out on people's names, once telling her he wanted to talk to "That farmer that lives halfway up the Island". Within seconds she had him connected to the exact person he had been thinking of.

The big wooden box in our porch was eventually replaced with a smaller wooden box with a black, one-piece handset which was sensibly relocated inside on the kitchen wall. Sometime around the end of the sixties, the Maritime Tel & Tel guys showed up, removed all the wooden phone boxes and replaced them with modern black plastic contraptions with a rotary dial on the front. Jerry Hoare of Digby was one of the phone company employees who switched all the phones on Digby Neck. He says they drove truckloads of the old wooden boxes to the dump.

With this massive change-over we reached the end of an era. The Islands had become one of the last places in Nova Scotia to be converted to dial phones, and the Freeport exchange was no longer needed.

Things have changed a lot since The Westport and Digby Telephone Company started up business in 1904, folding a year later after reaching a peak of fifteen customers. Today, we carry around in our pockets a phone that can do more things and handle more traffic than Elsie at her switchboard could ever dream of. Still, if some family emergency or community disaster got you out of bed in the middle of the night to make a phone call, there was something comforting and reassuring about hearing a human voice on the other end of the line.

It was nice to know that Elsie was there and that she was your connection to the rest of the world.

## 25: Big dogs and dental work

I have mentioned some of the doctors who have served the Islands. So many doctors have come and gone over the years that I can't remember them all; for instance, I have absolutely no recollection at all of Dr. Thomas. It was only while I was talking with my friend Jim Prime that his name came up. Jim remembers Dr. Thomas very well: when he was a boy, Jim had the unfortunate and painful experience of driving a large splinter under the nail of his big toe. Jim says he can clearly recall Dr. Thomas's young son sitting with his nose only inches away from his toe and watching in fascination while his father removed the offending sliver.

One doctor I do recall very well is Dr. Mink. I remember him mainly for two reasons. The first is for his love of dogs, big dogs. He had two slobbering, black Newfoundlanders that accompanied him everywhere he went, even on house calls. They would sit behind him in the back seat of his car, one or both of them with their head resting on his shoulder while he drove. This usually resulted in Dr. Mink arriving on his patient's doorstep with the lapel of his jacket displaying a less-than-attractive decoration of dried and dripping dog drool.

These dogs weighed in the vicinity of a hundred and fifty pounds each, and were generally friendly, but their large size did make them kind of intimidating, and any close encounter usually left you covered with flecks of flying slobber. Because of this, my sister Judy was a bit uncomfortable around these animals.

One summer's day, my mother took some of us kids over to the doctor's office in Freeport for our annual checkup. After sitting in the waiting room for a while, Judy, who was about six years old at the time, got bored and asked if she could go outside and play in the yard. A few minutes later, it occurred to me that the dogs might be outside, too, so I looked out the window to see if Judy was okay. To my surprise, she was standing in the yard right beside one of the dogs, calmly patting its head and talking to it, I was so amazed by this unusual sight that I called my mother over to have a look. The patting went on for several minutes until, finally, the dog walked away and Judy came back inside.

My mother mentioned to her that she was surprised to see her standing so close to the dog, since we all were under the impression that she was afraid of them. Judy replied that she *was* afraid of them. The reason she had stood there for so long was that the dog was standing on her foot and she didn't dare move it.

The second thing that I remember Dr. Mink for was his part in starting up the Freeport Sea Scouts troop. Apparently he had been involved in Scouting back in England, and thought it was an organization that the kids of the Islands could benefit from.

## Two Ferries Out

Sea Scouts is a marine version of Boy Scouts, and is supposed to provide ocean-oriented experiences for those who live near the water; although the only real sea-going experience I ever got in the year-and-a-half that I belonged to the group was on the ferry ride going to the meetings. As far as I know, I was the only Westporter to join the troop...not surprising, when you consider that the group met once a week through the winter months in Freeport on a school night. In order to attend, I had to eat supper early, rush down the road to catch the ferry across the passage, and then walk from Fish Point to the church hall on Crocker's Hill carrying my school books and a change of clothes for the next day. Since it would be dark by the time the meeting was over and the ferry stopped running at dark, my father had arranged for me to stay overnight at the home of Curtis and Elsie Prime, whose son Jim was also in Sea Scouts. The next morning, I would get up before daylight, have breakfast, walk back to the point as the sun was coming up, and catch the first ferry home in time for school in Westport.

This might sound like quite a bit of inconvenience and effort, but the fun we had at Sea Scouts made it worth the trouble. We earned badges for things like learning how to find our way through unfamiliar terrain using only a compass, how to build a shelter from tree branches, how to make a fire in the winter snow using a single match, and how to administer emergency first-aid. On cold or wet days, we continued to work on our badges back at the hall, mastering useful skills like how to tie a wide variety of knots and how to send semaphore messages with flags.

Dr. Mink usually brought his beloved dogs to these meetings, and would assign a different person each week to clean up after them. Since both dogs were massive droolers and didn't seem to be all that well housebroken, this was not a chore that anyone looked forward to. You didn't even get credit towards a badge for this job, which was a real shame, because the poor sap who was on duty the night the dogs ate something out of the garbage, and then threw up all over the floor, really did deserve some kind of award.

After Dr. Mink and his giant dogs left the island, Dr. Meehan was the next to arrive. Before coming to Canada, he had worked and lived in the Middle East with Mrs. Meehan, while the kids were back in England, attending boarding school. When they arrived in Freeport, it was the first time in quite a while that they had all spent any extended time together as a family. I think coming to the Islands in the middle of the turbulent sixties, with a family that included three teenagers, was a big adjustment and presented quite a challenge for them all.

Dr. Stokes was the last doctor whom I remember. He seemed to really take to the Island lifestyle, and appeared to have every intention of making it a permanent situation. Sadly, that was not to be. A few years after his arrival, Dr. Stokes' son was involved in a horrific highway accident that took the life of a young Island woman. A couple of years later, while responding to a medical emergency, Dr. Stokes suffered a fatal stroke behind the wheel of his Mini.

This sad event marked what was to be the final few years of doctor service on the Islands. Apparently, there were at least two more doctors: Dr. Westlake and then Dr. Boucher practised on the Islands for a couple of years each. But when the last of these left, it was the end of over a century of Islands-based medical service.

In addition to enjoying the services of an Island doctor, we also used to have occasional access to a dentist. For a few days every year, Dr. Julius Comeau would leave his office in Meteghan and set up shop in one of the front rooms at Lloyd's Hall in Freeport, bringing with him a portable dentist's chair and an antique drill rig that looked like it was barely one step above being powered by steam. This Rube Goldberg contraption was a complicated and intimidating combination of pulleys and belts, and it ran at such a low speed that you could almost count the revolutions of the drill bit as it slowly ground its way through your tooth enamel.

Because my father owned a store, and I had easy access to a wide variety of sugary drinks and snacks, I was probably more in need of Dr. Comeau's services than most kids. By the time I reached my middle teen years, I had already lost a couple of teeth due to cavities.

When I went back to him once again with a toothache, Dr. Comeau confirmed that I had yet another cavity, and commented that he could probably fix the tooth with a filling, but he might as well pull this one out, too. When I protested that I would rather keep the tooth if at all possible, he responded with surprise. It was the practise at the time, among many of the boys and even a few of the girls on the Islands, to scrupulously avoid visiting the dentist until they reached their mid-to-late teens. Then they would pay the dentist a visit and, in one fell swoop, have what was left of their teeth removed and get themselves fitted with a set of shiny new dentures.

Dr. Comeau was amazed to learn that I was interested in keeping as many of my own teeth as possible, and I was both astounded and appalled to realize that for the past few years he had been working on my teeth under the assumption that my ultimate goal was to make room for a set of store-bought choppers!

## 26: Roadwork

The weather on Brier Island is tempered by the sea. Summers can be a constant revolving door of hot sunny days, followed by several cool, foggy ones. Winter can bring vicious snow storms that are, more often than not, followed by rain and mild weather that quickly melts the snow.

This constant jumping back and forth across the freezing mark usually brings a spring full of frost heaves, broken pavement and potholes. As annoying as it might be to have your front wheel drop unexpectedly into an asphalt crater that just appeared overnight, the roads today are still better than they were before pavement brought the Islands another step closer to the age of modern transportation.

Sixty years ago, before the paving crews finally found their way down Digby Neck, a simple trip up the Island could be an ordeal for both man and machine. Back then, driving challenges changed with the seasons.

In winter there would be frozen ruts to contend with. It was not unusual to get several days of thaw in mid-winter, allowing axle-deep furrows to be plowed into the soft mud. Then, once these ruts were nicely formed, a cold snap would freeze them solid, creating an icy spider-web of intersecting tire tracks. A driver trying to negotiate his way through this slippery maze, would try to pick the most likely-looking ruts to follow. It was important to choose the correct set of grooves, because once you committed the car to a certain set of ruts, it was often difficult, if not impossible, to get out of them again. Occasionally, you would be forced in a direction you didn't necessarily want to go, like towards the ditch. Sometimes, the frozen ruts would diverge, causing the front wheels of your car to try to go in opposite directions, and the car to shimmy frantically from side to side, as if trying to decide which wheel to follow. Not exactly great for your wheel alignment.

In the springtime, all cars became the same shade of mud brown as warmer weather brought large, murky, puddles, easily big enough to provide a home for the Creature from the Black Lagoon. There were also several recurring "soft spots" that, year after year, ate up truckloads of gravel, but never seemed to get any firmer. Drivers would slowly zig-zag back and forth across the road, trying to pick a fairly solid route that could get them through to the other side of the soft spot and back on solid ground again without sinking up to the rocker panels.

Summertime brought drier roads, but drier roads brought dust and flying stones. It was far from unusual to see broken headlights, cracked windshields, or even a punctured radiator caused by rocks thrown up by passing traffic. If the weather was dry, a swirling cloud of dust followed each car, and covered every surface and every passenger in a gritty film. Driving behind a car on a dusty road was

## Two Ferries Out

like driving in the fog: you just concentrated on the taillights in front of you. If it was wet, the roads were greasy, and every time another car passed in the other direction, you would be momentarily blinded by a muddy spray covering your windshield.

The Department of Highways did most of its road improvements during the summer months, but rainy fall weather would undo a lot of their efforts, with multiple ruts and potholes developing so it felt like you were driving over a washboard.

Dirt roads require a lot of year-round maintenance, and each island had its own roadmaster. For many years, Brad Delaney attended to the roads of Westport. His main piece of equipment was a Caterpillar tractor, basically a small bulldozer, which had a powerful diesel engine and ran on steel treads. In the winter, he could attach a snow plow to the front. The rest of the year it towed various pieces of road maintenance equipment.

To a young boy, the most interesting piece of machinery, next to the tractor itself, was the grader. This was a long, gangly, complicated-looking rig that was towed behind the tractor. It had a scraping blade in the middle, two wheels in the front, two taller wheels in the back and a small platform at the very back where an operator could stand. The operator was kept busy turning several adjusting wheels and cranks and manipulating a row of levers to fine-tune the blade as it scraped the gravel road. A unique, and interesting to us young kids, feature of this contraption was that the operator could lean the rear wheels over to the right or left, which made it look like it was crabbing sideways as it rolled down the road. The grader was a rare sight, only brought out a few times a year after the roads had reached a certain level of decrepitude, so it was exciting to see bumpy, potholed dirt roads transformed into nice smooth, gravelled streets.

Most of the kids on the island lived within walking distance of the school, so we would walk home at lunchtime. One day, Chester Lent and I were on our way back to school near the end of our lunch hour when we paused to watch the grader at work. Finding the way the blade made a neat little ridge of dirt in the middle of the fresh new gravel to be utterly fascinating, we decided to follow it for a while. We were in no hurry, as afternoon classes wouldn't start for a while yet.

We trailed the grader down the back road and up the front, mesmerized by the footprints we were leaving in the smooth, freshly-turned gravel. When we rolled past the schoolhouse, the operator told us it was time to stop following him, and go back to school. We decided he was probably right, and that afternoon classes were most likely ready to start.

When we presented ourselves at the schoolroom door, we were surprised to see that we were a bit late and that classes had already begun. We sincerely explained to our teacher, Mrs. Garron, the perfectly legitimate excuse that we were late because we had been following the grader. She just sighed, and said that we might as well come in and take our seats.

Assuming we were only a few minutes late, we sat down and were just getting out our books when the bell rang. School was over for the day! We had spent the whole afternoon transfixed by the operations of the road grader.

A couple of times a summer, usually right after the roads had been graded, a tanker truck would arrive on the Island and spray the roads with a dark, oily substance that was supposed to help keep the dust down. We didn't think much of it at the time, but they were spraying hundreds of gallons of used oil on the road. Years later, it was revealed that there was a possibility that the chemical cocktail they had used included transformer oil, or PCBs, now considered a hazardous material. A small spill of this product today, is treated as an environmental and human health disaster that specially equipped biohazard teams have to handle.

For many years, Brad's Caterpillar tractor was the most powerful machine on the Island. If you needed a piece of equipment moved, a snowdrift pushed aside, or a car pulled out of the ditch, Brad's tractor could do it. It was a very rare situation that couldn't be resolved with the brute strength of that diesel engine. But I happened to witness one of those rare occasions when Brad and his machine were forced to admit defeat and give way to an older technology.

In those days, a few of the older fishermen who no longer wished to take on the difficulties and dangers of fishing in bad weather would haul their boats up onto the safety of dry land for the winter. One fall day, my twelve-year-old self was watching in fascination as a group of men struggled to get one of these boats up the beach. Several men were positioned on either side of the hull, balancing it on its keel, while Brad and his tractor pulled from the bow.

Unfortunately, things were not going well. The beach was fairly steep at this spot and covered with flat stones. The steel tractor treads were slipping and spinning, and the boat was not budging. This futile struggle had been going on for some time, and the tired and increasingly-frustrated men were shouting helpful, and some not so helpful, suggestions at Brad, who was constantly jogging back and forth, trying to get some traction.

Then, Gerald Morrell happened along with his team of oxen. He stopped to see what all the commotion was about, and some of the men suggested that he get a chance to see if his animals could do a better job of it than Brad and his tractor. Brad was, of course, skeptical. If his machine couldn't move this boat, then no animal was going to be able to do it. But, after a few more unproductive attempts, and more derisive shouts from the crowd, he reluctantly unhitched his tractor, and Gerald hooked the oxen up in its place.

As I watched these huge animals, it soon became apparent that they knew exactly what they had to do. Once their harnesses and lines were hooked up to the boat, you could see them lean into the yoke, testing the weight and getting a sense of what kind of load they had to pull. They shuffled their steel-shod feet, striking sparks as they looked for solid footing among the beach rocks.

Gerald patiently stood and waited, giving his team the time they needed to get ready. Then he quietly spoke a command and lightly flicked their rumps with his whip.

As a couple of thousand pounds of oxen put their weight into the job, you could hear the creaking and straining of the leather yoke straps and the grinding of the beach stones under their hooves; but the boat barely moved.

Brad was watching from the seat of his Caterpillar, and had just uttered a smug, "I told you so," when the pair paused, repositioned themselves, lowered their heads, and then lunged forward, bringing the boat with them. Muscles rippling, tails switching, nostrils steaming, they took one step, then another, and then, without stopping, Gerald shouting and encouraging them on, they went straight up the beach, across the road, and into the field.

Amid the cheering of the relieved group, Gerald just smiled, unhitched his team and continued on his way.

**Ben Robicheau**

*Westport Academy*

## 27: Westport Academy

In addition to memorable people, Brier Island also had a few notable buildings, such as the Baptist Church on the New Lane, which has recently been re-purposed into an arts centre. For over a hundred years, its spire has towered over the community, visible for miles around. Seamen used it as a marker as they navigated the treacherous waters around the Islands.

Another interesting building is the community centre on the Back Road, which is the only building in town that has a stage. Completed in 1910 as an Odd Fellows Hall, it was constructed using a cargo of lumber salvaged from the ship *Aurora*, which ran aground at Cow Cove in 1908. Apparently, church-spire navigating didn't work out too well for the *Aurora*.

When I was a child, the most important building I could imagine was the school house. For more than a hundred years, it stood there on the Back Road, a solid, some might say imposing, structure, resplendent in its coat of red-painted wooden shingles and with two tall rows of small-paned windows looking out over the village. For some, it was a place of opportunity and excitement, a place for learning and exploring and socializing. For others, it was nothing more than a dungeon, a boring routine of daily torture, where they grudgingly marked time on a hard, wooden seat until that happy day when their physical presence there would no longer be legally required.

The big, old, two-story building consisted of four large rooms, two on each side, separated by a central hallway topped with a bell tower. Back when the school was built, the Island population was larger and all four rooms were classrooms, with the grades Primary to Twelve divided up among them. But by the time I attended in the fifties, reflecting the shrinking population, one of the upper rooms had been converted to a rudimentary gym, and the grades were distributed among the remaining three rooms.

Louise Garron taught grades primary to four in the ground floor room on the "up-the-road" side of the building; Greta Swift, who had a reputation for not taking any foolishness from the new teenagers in grades five to eight, ruled over her room across the hall; and Helen Welch presided over the "big kids" upstairs in grades nine to twelve.

As I climbed up the well-worn granite steps on my first day of school, I experienced mixed feelings of excitement and apprehension to be joining the other kids behind the old, green door with the well-worn brass handle and thumb-latch. One of the first things I noticed upon entering was the big, black, cast-iron, pot-bellied stove that dominated the centre of the room. The back part of the porch that I had just passed through on my way in was actually a coal bin, where the fuel to heat the school was stored, piled up in dusty burlap sacks. In the winter, the school janitor would have a roaring fire going by the time we got to school, and throughout the day one of the high-school boys from upstairs would restoke to the fire at recess and noon.

On the coldest and windiest winter days, the old stove would sometimes get cherry red in its attempt to heat the farthest reaches of the draughty old classroom. With most of one wall made up of heat-sucking windows, twelve-foot ceilings, no insulation to speak of, and a floor that had cracks between the boards big enough to swallow your ruler or even your pencil, students seated close to the stove would roast, while those near the windows would shiver with the cold.

Coming in after a recess of frantic tunnel-building or a rousing snowball fight, we snow-covered kids would strip off our sodden snow suits and heavy winter coats and hang them to thaw and drip on the line of hooks across the back wall, and then arrange our wet mittens and boots on the sheet of tin that covered the floor around the hot stove. In short order, the room would fill with the unmistakable odour of wet wool and overheated bodies; you could sometimes actually see clouds of steam rising from the damp clothes of those students sitting nearest the stove.

The old stove was a source of fascination, with its iron door in the front where the coal was fed in; the long black stovepipe that went straight up and then, suspended from the ceiling by wires, ran along high above the teacher's desk and out through the wall; the coal scuttle and shovel that sat by the stove; the shiny brass decorative ring that circled the top edge of the stove; and the little cracks and gaps through which you could see the flickering flames, were all endlessly interesting to a little kid.

The bigger kids liked the old stoves, too. Every once in a while, when the teacher wasn't looking, someone would flip an eraser onto the hot top of the stove and the resulting stench of burning rubber would cause a brief evacuation. If the weather wasn't too bad, everyone would be herded outside while the teacher opened a window to air out the room; if it was too cold or rainy, they would just huddle in the porch, or go into the central hallway for a while.

I was shocked when I returned to school after summer vacation one year to find a nondescript brown metal box sitting in the middle of the classroom. The old coal-burner had been replaced with an oil stove; modern times were catching up with Westport Academy.

Well, maybe not all that modern, after all: there was still no running water in the building. Every morning, one of the older boys would go over to the Parsonage next door and bring back a pail of water for the metal cooler that sat on a shelf in the corner of the room.

One ritual that I always looked forward to was the morning line-up to take our daily, school-issued dose of cod liver oil. The teacher had a huge jar of cod-liver-oil capsules. She would pour some of them out into the lid, then place the lid on the corner of her desk where we would each pick up a capsule and a paper cup as we lined up to make our way to the cooler. Most of my classmates hated cod liver oil, but I loved the taste of it, and I could be easily persuaded to help some of the others out by chewing up their capsules as well as my own.

The lack of plumbing in the building also made bathroom breaks kind of interesting. Our "boys' and girls' rooms" were side-by-side outhouses out behind the school. The school outhouses were a step above the usual in that an enclosed runway attached them to the building, so we were afforded the luxury of not having to go outside to get to them. Because they were unheated, in the winter you generally didn't use the bathroom unless you absolutely had to, and then you usually took care of business as fast as possible to avoid the chance of frostbite in some tender and embarrassing areas.

In the yard on the primary grade side of the building there was a playground. It was the only semi-professionally constructed playground on the island, and we kids thought it was pretty good at the time, but most parents today, and probably a few parents even back then, would most likely be horrified to let their kids play there. There wasn't a lot of equipment, but the few pieces we did have were solidly built, and had the added attraction of being potentially dangerous.

The teeter-totter consisted of a twelve-foot, two-by-eight plank, balanced on a galvanized steel-pipe fulcrum. When you were on the "up" side of this, you were about five feet off the ground. One of the great playground pranks was to get some unsuspecting kid up in the air, and then keep him there, then, even better—or worse, depending on your perspective—jump off and let him crash to the ground. There are probably several people walking around right now with compressed spines because of this. They most likely would be a couple of inches taller if they had never fallen victim to the Westport Academy teeter-totter scam.

**Ben Robicheau**

The other major attraction was a swing set where you could get up some really great speed. The objective was to swing as high as the bar to which the swing chains were attached, on the theory that it was possible to swing right around the bar. There was a legend that some of the "big kids" had managed this amazing athletic feat, and though many of us smaller kids tried very hard to match this achievement, as far as I know it was never accomplished.

During inclement weather, the older kids spent their recess and noon times in the upstairs gym, playing basketball or volleyball, or maybe a bit of badminton. But as soon as the weather warmed up, the activities moved outside and consisted mainly of playing softball on the road in front of the school.

During his high-school years, Gary Frost managed to knock out more than a few school window panes in his attempts to hit another one of his famous home runs. One of Gary's more memorable homers created a minor mystery for our classroom. I was sitting in class one spring day when a red, white and blue-striped rubber ball crashed through the window, ricocheted off the top of Mrs. Swift's desk, and mysteriously disappeared into the far corner of the room. We searched fruitlessly for the vanishing ball for several days, until someone chanced to notice it jammed between the wall and a table leg.

When the new Westport school opened, Vic Strickland bought the old building to use as a workshop and as storage for all his odds and ends. Later on, an American who seemed to intend turning it into apartments bought it. He made a good start, painting and fixing up the exterior, but then seemed to lose interest, and the building gradually began to deteriorate again.

For several years, there appears to have been some doubt about who owned the building, and it fell farther and farther into disrepair. Then a group of forward-looking people on the Island started to work towards turning it into a museum. They made progress and collected artifacts, and it looked like the big red building might continue to hold a useful and valuable position in the community.

Sadly, this was not to be. Just when so many people were putting forth an effort to save a piece of island history, all their work, plans and hopes went up in smoke when the building was deliberately burned to the ground. The Island had, in one reprehensible and pointless act of vandalism, lost both a symbol of its past and a benefit to its future.

**Ben Robicheau**

*Pea Jack Road*

## 28: The Great Christmas Tree Hunt

For us kids, one of the best traditions of the old Westport Schoolhouse was the annual Christmas Tree Hunt. A week or so before Christmas break, a group would venture out into the wilderness in search of the perfect tree to adorn the classroom. Since the hunt took place during school hours, and therefore was a rare, officially-sanctioned day off from the gruelling everyday grind of lessons, recess and reading, there was always fierce competition to be included.

In those innocent days before we became aware of the existence of such a thing as sexual inequality, the oldest boy in the highest grade in the room would work hard to persuade Mrs. Garron or Mrs. Swift (depending on whether you were in the grades P to 4 or the 5 to 8 room) that he really did need every boy in his class to come along. This argument appears to have been surprisingly convincing, because the teachers always agreed.

Proper attire for this venture usually included rubber boots with heavy socks, long johns or insulated pants, and your brand-new winter coat. The wearing of mittens and a toque were optional, depending on the weather, and how nerdy you dared to look. Invariably, someone would forget that today was Tree Hunt Day, and would foolishly arrive dressed for a day sitting in an overheated classroom instead of for tramping around in the woods.

Although they sometimes regretted it after a few hours of wet feet and freezing fingers, this oversight usually wouldn't deter them from joining in, and we would all set out, armed with hatchets, saws and various other implements of destruction, under what we imagined were the envious and admiring gazes of the lower grades, in search of the sacrificial tree.

Our preferred routes to the tree-hunting grounds were usually the easiest and most obvious, up the New Lane to Western Light Road, or, if the snow was not too deep, straight across the fields behind the school, up the hill and into the woods. No matter which path we chose, there would usually be at least a few inches of snow to slog through, occasionally as much as a foot or more, and no matter what the weather, there always seemed to be fields of long, wet grass wicking your boots and pant-legs, and thickets of soggy alders trying to tear holes in the sleeves of your new winter coat.

More often than not, within a few minutes of entering the woods, we would find a perfectly acceptable tree. Of course, we would not cut this tree. This was partly out of the traditional belief of Christmas Tree hunters everywhere that, no matter how nice this tree was, a much better one was out there just waiting to be found.

But mainly, we didn't cut it right away because we weren't foolish enough to waste a day off from school by getting a tree and arriving back before the last possible minute. We would therefore happily spend the balance of the school day tramping through the brush, getting progressively wetter and colder, pretending to be looking for an ideal tree that we all knew we would never find.

As the day wore on, we would entertain each other with dirty jokes that most of us really didn't understand, eat our chocolate bars and chips, and drink the glass bottles of Coke that the more prepared of us had thought to stuff our pockets with, and constantly reinforce in each other the belief that, despite runny noses, numb feet and slowly but steadily-increasing cases of uncontrollable shivering, we were having a much more enjoyable time than those poor saps we had left back at the school.

Eventually, the joke-telling would devolve into an endless debate over whether we had been out long enough to take maximum advantage of our time away from school. By mid-afternoon, the lowering sun and a resulting discernible decrease in temperature would spur us on to a consensus in this matter, and, to the relief of most of us, we would come to the conclusion that it was finally time to harvest our tree.

This usually started another heated debate about the proper way to cut down a Christmas tree. Some argued a saw was the ideal tool; others favoured the axe. Still others thought you should just cut down the tree with whichever implement worked best, and then saw off the trunk to get the right height and leave a nice straight base for attaching the stand, usually the end of a wooden fish packing box held on with a couple of ten-penny nails.

The most radical tree harvesting method I ever heard of was from Gary Haines of Freeport, who claims that while out rabbit hunting one December, he came across the perfect tree. Not willing to take a chance on losing it to someone else, and lacking either axe or saw, he felled the tree with a few well-placed rounds from his 12-gauge shotgun, giving a whole new meaning to the term "Christmas Tree Hunt".

Finally, satisfied that we had milked the maximum amount of "fun" out of our day, we wearily tramped our way back to the schoolhouse. If we had timed everything correctly, we would be arriving triumphantly back at school, half-carrying-half-dragging our hard-fought-for prize, just a few well-timed minutes before the dismissal bell, wet, tired, just seconds from hypothermia, and most likely, with the very same tree that we had first seen upon entering the woods several hours earlier.

Despite the admiration our tree usually received from the other students, our heroic return, and our self-satisfaction at having cleverly scammed the school system out of a free day off, our triumph was somewhat mitigated by our discovery that, while we were out in the wilderness getting slapped in the face by wet branches and enduring cold, hunger, and (if truth be told) several long hours of boredom, the girls of the class, as well as those few boys who were not interested in tree hunting—those "poor saps" we had left behind—had not spent the day in monotonous drudgery as we had imagined. Instead of poring over math problems, or spending tedious hours reading about the mundane adventures of Tom and Betty and their unremarkable dog, Flip, it appeared that they had spent the day preparing the classroom for Santa's arrival.

The coloured chalk and Christmas stencils had been brought out, and the chalkboards were now bordered with red and green drawings of holly and lacy white snowflakes. The room was criss-crossed with construction-paper chains, also in traditional Christmas colours. Stencils and cans of spray snow had been applied to the windows that stretched across one wall of the room, and the small panes were each decorated with snowy images of candy canes, bells, trees, snowmen, and angels. There was even evidence that hot chocolate, gingerbread cookies, and other traditional Christmas treats had been consumed.

This was always a wonderful part of the school year, second only to the last day before summer vacation. For all intents and purposes, school work was over for the term. That other great school tradition, the Christmas concert, was only a day or two away. Then came blessed relief and release in the form of the Christmas break, and then the great day itself. The anticipation was almost unbearable!

The old, red Brier Island schoolhouse is long gone, and the more modern school that replaced it has, itself, been closed for many years now. All students from both islands now attend Islands Consolidated School in Freeport. I don't know if the students of I.C.S. go out to hunt trees for their school, or even if schools allow real trees in the classrooms any more, but my years of participation in the fine old tradition of the Great Christmas Tree Hunt is a memory that I will always keep.

## 29: The little house out back

I was born just at the end of the outhouse era. No, I'm not talking about the Long Island Outhouses, I mean the little-house-out-back outhouse, also known as the biffy, the one-holer, the privy, as well as by a few other, more explicit, labels. Because the house I grew up in had been converted to indoor plumbing a couple of years before I was born, I unfortunately missed out on all of the novelty and romance of having to go out in the dark and slog through wind, rain, and knee-high snowdrifts just to pee.

Actually, to be truthful about it, only half of the house had been converted. It was a two-family home and the other side still had a little room in the back porch that contained a bench with two holes in it. I'm not sure why it could accommodate two; maybe attending to bodily functions used to be more of a communal thing. I imagine that having this inside accommodation, and not having to go outside to make a forty-yard dash to the john when you were hit by a sudden onset of the green-apple-quickstep, was probably considered quite a luxury back in the day.

My grandparents lived in that part of the house for several years, and although I'm sure it was considered the height of modern convenience when it was installed, for the most part they didn't take advantage of their two-seater. They just came over to our side and used the more up-to-date facilities. But the little room in the back porch was still available for the occasional emergency.

Of course, the exception to plumbing advancements, as I previously mentioned, was the local school. By the time I started school in the early fifties, most of the houses in the village had long since been converted over to indoor plumbing, so I and most of my classmates were not exactly familiar with the intricacies of outhouse etiquette. To me, the big old red schoolhouse was one of the most impressive buildings in town. Surely this majestic monument to higher learning would have all the conveniences our modern age could offer. However we became intimately acquainted with this passé practise. There was no running water in the building and, therefore, no plumbing. What passed for bathrooms were in a small building behind the school, ominously topped off with several louvred "stink vents". There was no heat to this little building, and the several slotted vents in the walls and roof, designed to carry away any noxious odours, guaranteed that the temperature inside was pretty much the same as it was outside. I'm not sure if the designers of this building just didn't give any serious consideration to the comfort, health and safety of the students who were going to be using this miracle of last-century engineering, or if it was deliberately made uncomfortable to prevent any "lollygagging".

## Two Ferries Out

Years after modern plumbing and a growing recognition of the importance of personal hygiene had made the last of the outdoor bathrooms obsolete among the general population, we moved into the new Westport school where we finally got to partake of the modern luxuries of flush toilets, being able to wash our hands, and the novel experience of using the facilities without being distracted by snowflakes settling on your head or the bees buzzing around your knees.

The decommissioning of the school biffies meant there were only two outhouses left in town that I was aware of. One belonged to Myrna Garron. Located just a few convenient steps from her back door, it was a relic that had, by this time, been long relegated to the role of conversation piece, a quaint reminder of the past. The only regular use it got was when teenagers ritually tipped it over every Halloween night.

The only other outhouse, and probably the last functioning outhouse in the village, was a narrow little building located on the very edge of the property of what used to be known as the Coggins House, and right beside a dirt road known as Daniel's Lane. My father owned the Coggins House and used it as a residence for some of the men who came over from time to time from the French Shore to work at his fishplant. Eventually, an inside bathroom was installed and the outhouse, like its brethren before it, fell into disuse.

**Ben Robicheau**

One fine spring day, Dad decided that the yard around the house was in need of a clean-up and the by-now-decrepit old outhouse needed to go. He thought this would be a good project for me to take on, and I decided that the most economical and convenient way to get rid of an old and smelly outhouse would obviously be to burn it.

It was a hot day and the gasoline that I splashed around the inside of the windowless little house and up the back of the door, vaporized almost immediately. I closed the door and splashed the rest of the gas on the outside, stood back a few feet and tossed a match on the gas-soaked door. A barely-visible flame shot up to the top of the door and disappeared.

I expected the building to burst into flames, but for several seconds there was nothing. I was just thinking I should probably add some more gasoline when suddenly there was a terrific explosion! I could feel the concussion as the walls flew away in different directions, the roof came off and landed upside-down in the middle of Daniel's Lane, and part of what may have possibly been a burning toilet seat whizzed past my head.

I instinctively ducked to avoid the flying debris, and when I looked up again, the vision of an irate Gladys Bailey appeared through the slowly clearing smoke and dust, standing in her yard thirty or forty feet away amid an array of smoking and smouldering outhouse remnants. Now, you might think that Gladys would be out there to thank me for the good job I did in removing an eyesore from her neighbourhood, but no, all she seemed concerned about—and she was making very sure, in no uncertain terms, that I knew about this concern—was the heart attack I had apparently nearly caused her to have!

At one time, most of the fishermen's buildings that line the waterfront, referred to locally as "fish shops", had a little room somewhere in the back that usually contained nothing more than a wooden bench with a hole in it. It was a very basic and efficient operation: you made a deposit, and nature's plumbing system flushed it away with the next tide. Even in this modern time, there are still a few of these primitive but functional conveniences remaining.

The old wooden outhouse was just a little nondescript building, with a not-very-glamorous function, but it was a functional and necessary part of daily life. It did its duty well over the years, and when its work was done, I personally got to send at least one of them out in a blaze of glory!

**Ben Robicheau**

*Sunday School Concert*

## 30: Island Christmas traditions

The Great School House Christmas Tree Hunt was only one of the Island Christmas traditions. Another one that comes to mind is the Christmas concert. Most kids on the Island could look forward to being involved in at least one, or possibly both, of the two concerts that were held each Christmas season.

The first was the school concert, which was usually held in the Oddfellows Hall because that building had a proper stage. It even had a real curtain that slid on a wire and could be opened and closed. Everyone in the school would take part in this production in some way or other. We would put weeks of effort into the presentation of skits, songs, recitations and sometimes even a full-fledged play.

One year the grades 9, 10, 11 and 12 students, the "upstairs" grades in the old school, put on "A Christmas Carol" complete with sets, costumes and what to us smaller kids seemed to be amazing special effects. The clearest memory I have about that production is that the tallest kid in the school was picked to play Ebeneezer Scrooge, and every time he went through a doorway his top hat was knocked off.

The other big event of the season was the Sunday School concert. This took place in the church vestry and was similar to the school concert, except that there was not as much rehearsal time available. Plus, it included pre-school-age children, so the production values were often not up to the high standards we had come to expect from the school group's effort. I remember Sunday School teacher Etta Webber heroically trying to usher a dozen fidgety little pre-school age kids through a re-enactment of the Nativity story, patiently coaching and prompting from the sidelines, trying to feed the distracted little actors their lines as they stood mutely on the stage, or stared off into space, or just randomly wandered away into the audience.

Even though it may have suffered a bit quality-wise, we always anticipated the Sunday School concert with great excitement. You could never be quite sure what was going to happen. At some point in the evening, the twitchy little kid who was standing with her knees squeezed together might announce to the assembled masses, "I've got to pee!" causing her mother to spring from her pew, dash to the front of the room, snatch her baby off the stage and rush out the door, all the while trying to protect her good Sunday coat by holding the by-now-bawling child out in front of her like a sack of wet potatoes. The other parents accompanied her hasty exit with "been there, done that" chuckles. Sometimes, if the parent was paying close enough attention and was fleet enough, this dramatic rescue mission would succeed, but more often than not the other kids were left to carefully tip-toe around a suspicious-looking puddle on the little raised platform that served as a stage.

## Two Ferries Out

The highlight of the evening, of course, was the much-anticipated arrival of the old man himself, Santa Claus. After a lot of thumping on the door, stomping on the vestibule floor, sleigh bell ringing, and ho-ho-hoing, Jolly Old St. Nick would make his grand entrance into the Vestry Hall...where he would be greeted by the sight of several red-faced little kids running screaming to the safety of their mothers' laps. The rest of the children were usually all revved up in anticipation of the candy and presents to come, and Etta would have to take a firm hand to get things back under control.

Once Santa was safely seated, everyone would line up to take a turn on his knee and receive their treat and gift. Even the little ones, once they realized that presents and candy were available, could usually be persuaded to trade mom's lap for a few moments in Santa's.

When both of these concerts were over, you knew that you were well and truly into the Holidays. The only thing left now was the Big Event itself, Christmas Eve, followed of course by Christmas Day, and this brings us to another Island tradition.

Actually, I don't know if this really qualifies as a tradition, because it wasn't a formal event and it was mostly teenage girls who carried it out. I became aware of it sometime in the early sixties, but I'm not sure how or when it started, how long it went on for, or if it is something that still continues to this day.

The commencement of this tradition would be heralded about mid-afternoon of Christmas Day by the appearance of young teenage girls, usually in pairs or small groups of three or four, on the streets. Once all of their own presents were unwrapped and arranged for display under the tree, it was time to go out and "see the neighbour's trees".

School teacher Louise Garron was usually at the top of the visiting list. She always seemed to outdo herself each year with her spectacular and artistically arranged trees. One year she decorated her tree all in pink; another year it was an all-silver theme.

Although admiring and appreciating other people's trees was part of the reason for this venture, it was mainly an excuse to see what presents people had received. This definitely wouldn't qualify as a tradition if it was just kids going to see what other kids had received, but it was a bit more organized than that. Girls would arrange to go out together, then travel door to door in the days after Christmas, visiting friends, neighbours, young people, old people, anyone who would let them in.

The last tradition I'll mention is one that I know for sure actually is a tradition. As a little kid, I remember "Sandys" coming to our house in the days between Christmas and New Year. They were heavily disguised, usually dressed in old clothes, with their faces well covered, talking in strange voices or sometimes not talking at all. Often they would present themselves and just stand there in the kitchen, waiting while you tried to guess who it was under that disguise. Sometimes they sang, played an instrument, did a little dance or some other attempt at entertaining their hosts. My parents would carefully study the visitors, trying to recognize a piece of clothing or maybe get a glimpse of a facial feature that would tell them who this was; if they guessed correctly, the Sandyer might reveal himself.

For quite a while, I assumed that this was part of the universal Christmas celebrations and something that everyone, everywhere, did; but later on I discovered that most people off the Island had no idea what I was talking about if I mentioned Sandying, or Santa Clausing, as it was also known. I had to explain that, no, it wasn't like Halloween. Generally, only adults went Sandying, and there was no trick or treating involved, although refreshments, usually of the liquid variety, were sometimes offered. The participants didn't usually dress in costumes, but more often in disguises, the purpose being to hide their identity.

I began to think that this activity must be something that was unique to our Islands. Then I heard about a similar practice in Newfoundland called mummering or jannying that Irish and English settlers had introduced; then I later found out that some people on Prince Edward Island went out belsnickling over the Holidays. By now I had decided that this must be an old ritual that somehow had spread from island to island. Then I found out that in a few communities in the Lunenburg area of the South Shore, people still carried out the old German custom of belsnickling, which they also call Kris Kringeling.

**Ben Robicheau**

Even though these traditions go by a variety of names and have developed some differences in the way they are practised, it appears that mummering, belsnickling, and Sandying all stem from an ancient New Year's custom that the first European settlers brought to the New World. As time went on the custom gradually disappeared in a lot of areas, because inviting possible strangers whom you couldn't identify into your home, didn't seem like a good idea to most people; in some towns and cities, it was even outlawed.

The tradition survived longest in isolated places like the Islands, probably because even though you might not be able to identify your visitors, you could feel comfortable that there is no doubt that it is a neighbour, friend, relative, or even, in some cases, your husband or wife, who is standing in your kitchen, wrapped up in old clothes, and talking in a funny voice.

I never went Sandying myself. By the time I got old enough to go out, it had pretty much faded away; but a bit later on, there was a revival of the practice. One of my sisters tells about going out in a good disguise and not having anyone guess who she was, although one person came close, saying, "I don't know which one you are, but with those eyes you've got to be a Robicheau."

Let's hope that the conditions that have allowed this ancient tradition to live so long in our communities will continue and Sandying will be around for many more Christmases to come.

## 31: Holiday shopping

For most people, Christmas shopping today usually involves visits to any of a variety of specialty stores, trips to over-crowded, over-decorated malls, with too many choices on display, and, of course, we now have on-line sites, like Amazon, that give you access to unique items from all over the world right from the comfort of your own easy chair.

Shopping for that special gift presented a bit more of a problem on the Islands when I was a kid. Holiday shopping opportunities were a bit more limited, back when the Island roads were unpaved, the ferries stopped running at dark and a personal car was still a luxury item for many people.

Even if you did have a vehicle, it took up a good part of your day on barely-passable winter roads to get to Digby and back, and a shopping trip all the way to Halifax was a major expedition involving at least one overnight stay. Of course, those without their own transportation could still get to Digby by "going on the mail" which involved catching an early morning ride with Lloyd Blackford, or one of the people who followed in his footsteps over the years, as they carried the Island mail up to the Digby Post Office. Unfortunately, most of the day would be taken up with stops at every rural post office along the way, and you would end up with only an hour or so to do your shopping before it was time to climb back aboard Lloyd's bus for the return trip down the Neck.

For most of us, Christmas shopping back then was pretty much limited to two options. The first were the local stores, of which you had a much wider selection than you do now. There were Elliott's and Outhouse's stores in Tiverton, there was Pyne's in Central Grove, and Freeport had McIntyre's store, Norm Perry's store, and Curtis Prime's small but mighty corner store. Westport was a veritable shopping Mecca, with six stores in all. My father's store was across from the ferry wharf. Dick Welch had a store just a couple of doors down the street, Wilfred Swift ran the Co-op store a bit further down the road, and, in Irishtown, Mary Chayko had the retail area below the bridge all to herself. Bowers' Store was built out over the water at the bottom of The New Lane and, directly across from it in the building that now houses the only remaining store on the island, was Louey's.

Even though all the stores made a big deal at Christmas time by decorating their windows and stocking up on special food and gift items for the holiday season, the truth was that they all dealt mostly with the same suppliers and they all carried pretty much the same things. When you went out on Christmas and Boxing Day for the traditional checking-out of your friends' presents, you were pretty well guaranteed to see many of the exact same items under their tree that you had at home under your own.

Of all the stores, Louey's was your best bet for Christmas shopping. It was a bit different from the other stores on the Island. Louey's was a dry-goods store: no groceries, no boat anchors, no roofing nails here, just a quiet little store crowded with lots of things you couldn't find anywhere else. From the high counters and deep cubby-hole shelves along the walls you could buy cloth by the yard, a wide variety of ribbons, thread, and yarn, winter coats, puzzles, toys, magazines, china cup-and-saucer sets, pots and pans. You name it, Louey's had it.

There was a big side window looking out onto the New Lane that they decorated for special occasions, and at Christmas time it was always dressed up with Holiday decorations. You might even see your own special Christmas present-to-be on display there.

Louey's always brought in a few exotic items at Christmas time, but because they were usually a bit more expensive, they only got one or two of each. These items would be on display for all to see and admire, but in the weeks leading up to Christmas, one by one, they would slowly disappear from the window. For many of us kids, this would cause an uncomfortable mixture of anxiety and elation; on the one hand, disappointment, because it could mean that someone else had bought that one thing that you really, really wanted before you were able to work your Christmas magic and successfully convince your parents that you absolutely deserved to have it. Of course, on the other hand, excitement, because there was always the possibility that your magic had worked, and it was your parents who had bought it! Only on Christmas morning would you know for sure.

Although it was owned by the E.C. Bowers Company, and was really just an extension of the main grocery and hardware store across the road, everyone called it Louey's Store. Lulu (Louey) Repool was the clerk who had looked after business in the store for as long as most people could remember. I recall her as always being a little old lady, right from my very first memory of her. She was a very reserved, quiet person, whose main social activity seemed to consist of faithfully attending church twice a week. She lived in Irishtown, in a little house set off by itself at the end of the lane up past Cora Thompson's boarding house, with her brother Ray. Like his sister, Ray was short in stature, but he was the polar opposite in personality, loud and boisterous. He liked to regale anyone who would listen with stories about his wild and rambunctious younger days at sea and ashore, during the era of wooden ships.

Many people looked upon Louey's as the Macy's or Gimbels of the Island, their first choice for Holiday shopping.

The second shopping option for many was the "wish book", the special Christmas edition of the Eaton's or Simpson's catalogue that arrived every Fall. On the face of it, catalogue shopping was perfect for someone in an isolated area. You simply browse through the thousands of items in the book, choose and order the thing you like, and a short time later pick it up at the Post Office. Nothing could be simpler.

Well, in reality, it didn't work quite that smoothly. First, it was a commonly-held belief that all of the popular items were reserved for the big cities like Toronto and Montreal, and all of the out-of-date fashions and items that didn't sell elsewhere were sent off to the Maritimes. It always seemed that if you ordered anything that was currently at the top of the fashion charts, it would inevitably be out of stock. In fact, it seemed that you almost never got exactly what you ordered, no matter what it was! They would often substitute your order if they didn't have the exact item in stock. Usually, it would be last year's version of the same thing, or it would arrive in a less popular colour or style than what you had ordered.

Occasionally, you would get something completely and wildly unrelated to what you wanted. It almost seemed that, if something was out of stock, the warehouse guys would just choose something at random, on the off-chance that you could use it, and ship it out on the premise that, after you've waited six weeks for your order, getting anything at all was better than getting nothing. To an extent this was true.

Although the items always looked great on the glossy catalogue pages, you couldn't pick them up or feel the quality of the material or try them on, so you never really knew exactly what you were going to get even if, by some miracle, you did get what you ordered. Even though the catalogue contained several sizing charts and detailed instructions on how to properly measure yourself, getting clothes or shoes that actually fit was a hit-or-miss proposition. Often, an article of clothing would make several trips back and forth before the correct size was arrived at.

Mothers habitually over-estimated their children's sizes on the basis that it was better to get clothes too big because the kid would eventually grow into them. My sister Rikki once convinced my mother, after a long and intensive campaign, to order her a shirt that was all the rage among the fashion-conscious at the time. She waited in high anticipation for several weeks until the package from Eaton's finally arrived, Rikki tore it open and tried on her stylish top, only to find that it was two sizes too small. Despite a lot of pleading and begging, my Mother couldn't face all the hassle of returning it for the correct size, so the shirt went down the line of seven sisters until it came to one whom it would fit. Judy, who couldn't care less about fashion at the time, got a fabulous new shirt, and a disappointed Rikki got a replacement shirt from Dad's store, one just like what every other kid on the Island was wearing.

Today, people on the Islands have an easier time of it, as the roads and the ferry service have vastly improved. Just about everyone has a car, or access to transportation of some sort, and you can order nearly anything you can think of just by pushing a few buttons on your phone or with a few clicks of your computer mouse.

Modern technology has its benefits, and eBay and Amazon have long ago overtaken the now-defunct Eaton's catalogue, but I just can't see how staring at a computer screen can compare to the excitement and anticipation generations of Island kids felt as they pored over the "wish book" in those days and weeks leading up to an Island Christmas.

**Ben Robicheau**

*Clayton Titus's model of the "Miss T".*

## 32: Hand-made in Westport

One of the big parts of Christmas is gift-giving. Leading up to the holidays, people all over the country run frantically from store to store, searching for just the right present so they can finally cross one more person off their list. Then they select paper, ribbons and bows so they can wrap, decorate, and finally artistically arrange their purchases to make an impressive pile under the tree. On Christmas morning, all that careful folding and taping is quickly reduced to a red and green blizzard of flying scraps, and we end up knee-deep in colourful drifts of crumpled paper.

The vast majority of presents exchanged will most likely be manufactured in an anonymous factory in some distant land, but there will be a small percentage of this year's Christmas gifts that will bear no nylon tag saying "Made in China" or Thailand or India, they won't be encased in a plastic shell that's almost impossible to open, and they won't have a computer bar-code attached. Some of the most appreciated and treasured gifts are from someone who took the time to be creative with a pair of knitting needles or a sewing machine or a hammer and some lumber, producing a one-of-a-kind item with only you in mind.

**Ben Robicheau**

When I was eleven or twelve, one of the most sought-after items by young boys on the Island was a model boat. Frank Shaw was generally considered to be one of the finest model makers on the Island. From his shop in Irishtown he turned out some very high-quality work. There were others, usually fishermen who whiled away the stormy winter days building miniature replicas of the same boats that were bobbing up and down at their moorings in the harbour, everything from Cape Islanders to draggers to herring seiners, right down to exact copies of the punts and dories tied to their wharves.

All these years later, any of these models that were lucky enough to survive are most likely sitting in a place of honour on a mantelpiece or in a sunroom, maybe protected in a glass box, treated as a piece of art. That wasn't always the original intent. Many of these replicas were built to be toys to be played with, not objects to be put on display.

As kids, we did have some appreciation for the detailed artistry that the more skilled model-makers put into their work. They must have invested many hours in reproducing not only the boat, but miniature trawl tubs, anchors, oars, gaffs and a lot of the other little items you would find on a fishing boat. Some of the models were exact copies of specific boats and it was kind of neat to be sailing your boat among the seaweed-covered rocks of the shoreline and look up to see the full-size original floating in the harbour. Clayton Titus had a model of the "Miss T", the same boat that his father went fishing on.

## Two Ferries Out

It took a lot of time, and some considerable skill, to produce these "toys", but for the most part, all we kids were really interested in was did it look like the boats we were used to seeing, would it float properly, and how much "fish" (seaweed) would it carry.

As a child in Holland, my uncle, Ben Verburgh, had become interested in model-making. He moved to Canada after WWII, lived in Westport for a while, and learned a lot from Frank Shaw and the other model makers on the Island. He and his friend Donald McDormand honed their skills in Donald's father's fish shed. Benny says that Ace was quite tolerant of their interest in miniature-ship building; a bit surprising, considering that they carved the hulls of most of the ships they built from Ace's wooden lobster buoys.

My uncle took what he learned in Ace's shed and from the Island modellers, and turned it into a lifelong career. He worked for a while as a cabinetmaker at the Saint John Shipyard, where part of his job was to build models of ship interiors. He moved on to a job as model maker for the newly-opened Ontario Science Centre. His high-quality models of famous and historic ships are in museums all over the world.

After the snow fell, we put away the model boats and got out another home-made toy. It also was a miniature replica of a common Island item, but this one required much less time, skill and material to produce. Most of us kids were capable of building this one ourselves, no matter how rudimentary our carpentry skills,

All that we needed were a couple of trap laths, a hammer, a saw, and a few nails. First, we carved four short pieces of lathe roughly into the shape of runners, then added two more short pieces as front and rear supports for the runners, finally a longer piece of lathe would join the two units together, with the rear runners being solidly fixed and the front runners being attached with a single trap nail so they could swivel.

What you now had was a very basic model of a bobsled. After tying a piece of fishing line to the front set of runners and the other end of the line to a stick, you could walk along and guide your sled over the snowdrifts. It was not unusual after a snowfall to see lots of little parallel lines in the fresh snow along the side of the road.

One winter we got quite a bit of snow, and it stayed around for several days. This was unusual for Bier Island because the temperatures there tends to be milder than on the mainland, so snow doesn't usually last long. This abundance of the white stuff spurred me in the attempt to build myself some winter equipment, without much success, as it turned out.

Someone had got a pair of skis for Christmas, and they looked like they were having a lot of fun with them on Joe's Hill, so I thought I would also like to take up skiing. Christmas had just passed by, and my birthday wasn't for another ten months, so it didn't look good for getting skis as a gift. Besides, chances were pretty good that my father would look at any request from someone who lived on Brier Island to spend good money on skis as the height of foolishness. After all, the Island is noticeably lacking in mountains, a basic requirement for making any real use of downhill skis. But we did have Joe's Hill: far from a ski run, but enough of a slope that you could experience at least a few seconds of the skiing experience. Assuming you had skis, which I didn't.

As I mulled over my problem, it occurred to me that barrel staves are sort of shaped like skis, and that, as it happened, I was aware of the location of an old barrel that had fallen apart after the steel retaining rings had rusted away. After yanking out a couple of suitable-looking staves, I cut a few pieces of cod line out of an old, retired trawl and nailed these to the staves. This would do as bindings to attach my feet to the skis.

Next, I needed poles to go with my skis, and I knew just where to get them. The old smoke house on the wharf behind my father's store was full of bundles of "herring stringers", long, thin poles to string fish on while they hung in the smoking racks. I selected a couple of these black, greasy, smoked-herring-smelling sticks and set off for Joe's Hill, my skiing ensemble now complete.

By the time I got to the top of the hill I was nearly exhausted. My skis were almost two inches thick and had obviously soaked up a lot of water over the years. They were quite heavy and I didn't look forward to lugging them up the hill again. But, standing on the top of Joe's Hill and observing the wide expanse of snow before me, I figured I would have so much fun skiing down that I probably wouldn't mind walking back up. To make sure that I didn't go too fast and too far, and possibly hit the fence at the far end of the field, I picked a spot on the hill that wasn't too steep for my first run.

After tying the cod lines around my boots, I stood up, set my herring stringer poles, and pushed off... except I didn't move an inch. I tried again, a little harder this time...still nothing.

Maybe I needed to be on a steeper section of the hill. I laboriously shuffled over to a better spot and tried again... same result. No amount of pushing or trying to slide my skis back and forth would get me going.

I ended up on the steepest section I could find, pushed with my poles and leaned as far forward as I dared. I felt like I was on an almost vertical incline, but nothing would make those skis slide. I could have been on the steepest slope in the Alps and it wouldn't have made a difference.

Who would have thought that making skis out of rough lumber that had been soaking in fish-pickling brine for forty years or so would turn out to be a bad idea?

I ended up stepping out of my cod line bindings and walking away. For all I know, the barrel-stave skis are still there on the side of Joe's Hill where I

## Two Ferries Out

stepped out of them, waiting for some other poor soul to give them a try.

Many years later, I was able to take another stab at skiing, but with proper equipment and on a real ski hill this time. I enjoyed it, and it was a lot of fun finally getting to zoom down the hill, but I'll never forget my first ski experience on Joe's Hill.

**Ben Robicheau**

## 33: Turkey, lobster, and pie—oh, my!

A holiday tradition that islanders enthusiastically share with the rest of the world, with a few local variations, is the Christmas/New Year's eating marathon. You would think that the act of preparing and consuming food would by now have become extremely boring and mundane to us. After all, it's a chore that we perform several times a day, each and every day of our lives. Yet, we are still able to get excited over food, and we use special meals as a way to mark important milestones in our lives.

The birthday or anniversary cake, the wedding reception meal, the big turkey feast at Thanksgiving, the family barbecue in the backyard, all serve to make a special occasion more memorable. If we want to show someone that we really appreciate them, or that we just enjoy their company, we do it by inviting them into our kitchen and making them something to eat.

Food-related celebrations are almost always group events where we get to share meals with friends and family or, at the very least, with that one very special someone. I can't think of any holiday that people celebrate by sitting and eating alone. I suppose this all relates back to the dawn of time when we were all hunter-gatherers and the term "bringing home the bacon" was taken much more literally. If you didn't manage to catch that big fish, or get that grizzly bear before it got you, or harvest that last bunch of berries before the snow fell, the consequences could be severe. Sharing what you had with one another must have meant even more to people in those days than it does now.

We do our most intensive celebrating over the Christmas holidays. Christmas Eve usually involves consumption of the traditional eggnog and other festive drinks, as well as a wide variety of special snacks and treats. Christmas Day itself, is the highlight of the holidays, featuring the big meal with all the trimmings: turkey with stuffing, mashed potatoes with gravy, and a variety of vegetables. Family favourites, like Aunt Rita's scalloped potatoes or Grandma's special Jell-o salad, come out for this special meal. And then, when you are sure you can't possibly eat another bite, we finish off the whole thing with a nice big slice of mincemeat pie.

Then, just a week later, we do it all over again to celebrate the arrival of the New Year. Many people go with the whole traditional menu again, pretty well duplicating what they had just managed to digest from the previous week, but some people like to mix it up a bit. For people on the Islands, substitutions or additions to the usual turkey main course might include lobster, a nice beef or pork roast, fish of course, and maybe some wild duck or venison that was still in the freezer from the last hunting season. In recent years, the trendy alternative to the standard Butterball in some areas has become the "turducken", a chicken stuffed inside a duck stuffed inside a turkey. I don't know if this food fad has made it to the Islands yet. I personally don't find it all that appealing, it just seems like it might be too much of a good thing.

Of course, on the Islands we have always had a bit of a different relationship with certain foods. As school kids in Westport, we were always able to go home for lunch (except for the lighthouse kids, who lived too far away at either end of the island), but when we started going to school across the harbour in Freeport, we had to bring packed lunches. Once lobster season rolled around, a lot of kids, of course, had lobster sandwiches in their lunchboxes. To someone from off the Island, who might pay big bucks for what they probably consider a rare delicacy, school kids bringing lobster sandwiches for lunch might seem like some kind of unbelievable luxury; but after the first week or so, any kid with a lobster sandwich would happily trade it for peanut butter, if he could find someone willing to trade. It is possible to get sick of too much of anything, even lobster.

When I was a little kid, some of the older people on the island were ashamed of the fact they had to eat lobster. At that time, the accepted method for getting rid of your garbage was to just toss it on the beach and let the tide carry it away. You could occasionally find lobster shells wrapped up in newspaper or hidden in boxes among the trash.

I asked my father why people tried to hide the fact they were eating lobster, and he told me that it was a holdover from the bad days of the Great Depression. Back then, if people didn't have enough money to buy store-bought food like hamburger or bologna, they would have to eat whatever was available for free. They didn't want their neighbours to know that they were so poor they had to eat whatever they could catch day after day, so they hid the evidence. This may well have been the reason that some people hid the lobster remnants, but I did notice that a lot of the shells looked kind of small, and I suspect that it was just as likely that they didn't want anyone to know they were eating jinks: undersized and illegal lobsters.

A really unique island food item is the egg tart. When you try to describe it to someone from away, they generally think you are talking about something like a quiche. After explaining that, no, this is a dessert tart made mainly of eggs, sugar and vinegar; you usually get some odd looks and comments to the effect that this particular combination of ingredients doesn't sound like it would be very good. But if you happen to have an egg tart in your possession and can get them to try it, you will most likely make another convert to the delicious local delicacy that is the Island egg tart.

I have never seen the Island-style egg tarts in any other place. While walking through Chinatown in

## Two Ferries Out

Toronto, I saw egg tarts displayed in a bakery window. They looked sort of like the egg tarts I was familiar with, so I bought one. I was sorely disappointed. It tasted slightly like an Island egg tart, but had more of a spongy, custard-type filling, without the sugary crunch and familiar vinegary bite of the Island tart. It turns out that there are Asian-, Portuguese- and English-style egg tarts, but they all are the custard style of tart. The Island egg tart, as far as I can tell, is the only one made with vinegar, and appears to be unique to our corner of the world.

Of course, I can't very well talk about Island food without mentioning fish! Sadly, the days when there were nearly a dozen fish processing plants on the two islands and you could just walk into any one of them and get yourself a mess of haddock or pollock fillets, cod tongues or cheeks from fish that were still flipping, are long gone. There was a time when no Islander worth his salt would even consider eating a frozen fish. Between the fishplants and the dozens of fishing boats moored in the harbour, you could have your choice of pollock, halibut, hake, haddock, or cod any day of the week, and at certain times of the year there were also mackerel and sometimes even tuna or wild Atlantic salmon to be had, as well as scallops when the Digby fleet was in the area.

Then there were the smoked fish, like Digby Chicks and Finnan Haddie. A visit to one of the fish driers could supply the basic ingredient for a salt fish dinner. Add some boiled potatoes, mashed turnip and a little diced, fried salt pork to your boiled salt fish, and you've got yourself a true Maritime meal. Some old-timers even used to carry a bit of dried salt fish in their pocket so they could bite off a piece any time they felt like a snack.

Sometimes the best meals are the most basic ones. When it is available, nothing beats a simple piece of fresh, pan-fried fish. For years, my Uncle Brian came to Westport on vacation from Ontario. He enjoyed visiting the Island, but would refuse to eat any fish, saying that he had tried it as a child in England and again as an adult in Toronto, and he didn't like it. My mother always replied that the problem was that he hadn't tasted *her* fish, and one summer she was determined to get him to try it.

On the last day of his visit, after a week and a half of pestering from my mother, Brian agreed to taste one piece of her fried fish. After the first piece, he ate another, then another and another until it was all gone. Properly cooked fish, fresh from the ocean, was such a revelation to him that he extended his vacation for several more days and kept my mother busy making more fried fish, baked fish, fish chowder, fish cakes; basically, anything involving fish. He couldn't believe what he had been missing all those years!

**Leona Delaney's Egg Tart Recipe**
(saved and passed on by Rikki Clements)
   4 eggs
   1 cup white sugar
   1 cup brown sugar
   1 tsp vanilla
   5 tbsp cider vinegar

Beat together but don't over-beat, as this makes them more like custard. They should have a foam on them when they go in the oven, though.

Pour into unbaked shells.

Bake at 325 until golden brown on top, about 20-30 minutes.

Keep checking so the crust doesn't burn, but make sure they are set.

**Ben Robicheau**

*Ready for lobster season.*

## 34: Halloween in Westport

Next to Christmas, the most anticipated day of the year was Halloween. For the smaller kids, Halloween was all about the candy. Within seconds of hitting the street, word would spread among the trick-or-treaters as to who was giving out the best treats. "Best" usually meant the biggest, or the most sugar-filled...with luck, both.

The main objective was to fill that loot bag! The most optimistic among us would set out with a pillow case or shopping bag to hold our anticipated stash of goodies. If you set your mind to it, you could fill it completely before the night was over. If you managed to fill it more than once, that was even better. A few kids would make the rounds, go home and dump what they had collected, change costumes, and go round again.

At the end of the night, we would pile up the collected goodies in the middle of the living room floor and sort them by order of desirability. Store-bought treats were usually at the top of the list; occasionally a few people would even give out regular items, like full-sized chocolate bars or boxes of Cracker Jacks. The miniature-sized bars and small packages of licorice were good, too. Home-made treats, like fudge, squares, cookies, and popcorn balls, could be high or low on the list, depending on who made them, and what flavour they were. Of this type of treat, for my money, the best could be found on the New Lane. If you made it to Mrs. Gaudet's house up the hill near the church before she ran out, she might treat you to a little brown-paper bag containing four of her delicious taffy candies; two molasses flavour, (my favourite) and two of the vanilla.

Then, sadly, there were those people who actually had the nerve to hand out items that could almost be considered healthy. Into this category fell things like bags of salted peanuts (or even worse, peanuts in the shell), little boxes of raisins and, at the very bottom of the desirability scale for most kids, fruit like apples or even the occasional orange or banana. Thankfully, these items usually took up a very small section of floor space, compared to the huge piles of chocolate, chips and various types of candy.

At the bottom end of the health scale was one item you could always depend on getting plenty of, whether you wanted it or not. The orange-and-black-wrapped Halloween chews were a gooey, sticky, candy concoction that, if you weren't careful, could suck the fillings right out of your teeth. I actually liked these candies, so I was happy to end up with a lot of them, many donated by friends with a little more discerning taste; although I found that after eating fifteen or twenty in a row, they tended to make you feel a little queasy.

As you got a bit older, Halloween became a little less about the candy and a little more about the costumes. At a certain age, it became important to try to come up with a cooler get-up than the next person. On Halloween day, you got to wear your costume to school, and there was sometimes even a prize for the best outfit.

This was in the days before there were a lot of store-bought costumes available, so either your mother had to spend a lot of time sewing something fancy, or you would put your imagination to work and come up with a disguise using everyday items. This usually resulted in a lot of hobos wearing their parents' old work clothes; ghosts draped in old bed sheets; and pirates with red or blue polka-dot handkerchief headscarves, folded-down rubber boots, and a sword whittled from a trap lathe stuck in a waistband made from a knitted winter scarf.

As we got into our early teen years, we would finally be old enough to join in the exciting tradition of "roughnecking". For some, there would be a bit of an overlap period here, when people would go out with the little kids trick-or-treating in the early part of the evening, then safely stash their candy at home before dumping the costume and joining the older kids out roaming the roads. Roughnecks were concerned mostly with the "trick" part of trick-and-treating. A few people in the village were either easy victims or willing participants, and regularly fell victim to the traditional pranks the roughnecks played on Halloween night.

The Canns had a picket fence around their house on the Front Road and, like clock-work, every Halloween his gate would disappear. Usually someone would find it the next morning hanging from a tree in the front yard of a near-by neighbour. Mr. Cann could have easily removed the gate every October 30 for a couple of days to avoid this, but he didn't. Maybe he enjoyed the tradition, too.

Outhouse tipping was another popular, traditional joke to play on people. By the time I was able to participate in this time-honoured prank, Myrna Garron had one of the last outhouses in town, and for several years good-naturedly endured the brunt of the Halloween toilet-tippers.

As soon as it got dark, the main endeavour was to make the roads impassable for any vehicle. This was accomplished by moving almost anything that could be carried, dragged, or pushed out into the road. On Halloween night, teenagers who were hard-pressed to find the energy to carry the groceries home for their mother during the day suddenly found themselves endowed with super powers that allowed them to construct incredible barricades as soon as the sun fell below the horizon.

On one of the first Halloweens when I was allowed to go out and join the older kids, a bunch of teenagers were moving an old double-ender fishing boat that had been hauled out of the water and left beside the road. It had been there for several years and it was clear that it wasn't ever going back to sea, so they decided it would make a great barricade. They lifted the old boat from its resting place and dragged it out across the road. The next morning, I happened to be passing by the spot on my way to

## Two Ferries Out

school, and stopped to watch as it was returned to its former location. Twenty men and a tractor struggled for half an hour to undo what a dozen kids had done in a few minutes the night before.

On another occasion, the kids built a great wall across the road in front of Bowers' store. They stacked the now-empty barrels that stove oil had been delivered in. The first couple of rows were no problem, but the rest were more of a challenge. At first, a couple of guys climbed up and balanced on the drums while the others passed up the barrels, by the time they were up to the third row, the guys on the ground had to swing the barrel back and forth between them and then toss it up, to be caught by the guys on top. They were tossing them up four or five rows high when they ran out of barrels; otherwise, who knows how high that wall would have been?

One year, Halloween fell right in the middle of a construction job going on at the lower breakwater. The material to rebuild the wharf was stored along the side of the road and the job manager (a mainlander) was warned about what might happen to all that lumber overnight. He stacked everything in neat piles, nailed boards across them, and left the Island that afternoon, feeling confident that everything was secure from whatever damage a bunch of trick-or-treaters might try to do. The next morning, he returned to find his entire inventory of twenty-four foot, ten-by-ten timbers stacked up log cabin style in the middle of the road. He took one look at his building material reaching up past the telephone wires and, in a most un-Island-like reaction, called the police.

It caused great excitement when the R.C.M.P. arrived at the school just before noon, pulled the grade eleven and twelve boys out of class, even those who had had no part in the prank, marched them all down the road, and made them disassemble the previous night's project.

Because islanders knew what to expect on Halloween, everybody left their cars at home, the stores closed early and, for the most part, adults stayed home. Even though all the kids worked hard to make it impossible to drive anywhere on the island, if an emergency arose or if a senior citizen found themselves caught on the road after dark, a passageway would be quickly cleared, usually by the same group who had blocked the road in the first place.

Of course, there were those who deliberately challenged the barricades. One year, David Pugh took his father's Jeep truck and tried to see how far he could get with it. He managed to crash and crawl around, over, and through several piles of debris, but the roughnecks rallied to the cause and worked even harder to block him in with bigger and higher walls. David did get the old truck an impressive distance up the road, but eventually had to give up when he acquired a couple of flat tires in the process.

Although it may appear as if Halloween night was a wild and crazy time when all the rules were thrown out, it wasn't quite as lawless as it sounds.

**Two Ferries Out**

Lobster season was just a couple of weeks away, and the wharves and roadsides were lined with traps, coils of rope, and piles of buoys. They might have been perfect barricade-building material, but fishing gear was off limits and left untouched. For the most part, the roughnecks left alone anything of value or necessary to someone's livelihood, and did very little real damage. Halloween was a night when the normal order of things was turned on its head for a few hours, but the next day everything was usually disassembled and put back where it should be in short order.

Then the planning would begin for next Halloween.

**Ben Robicheau**

*Peter's Island in winter.*

## 35: Lost at sea on Christmas Eve

*A story told from two points of view*

**Ben's experience**

It's a week before Christmas, 1969. I'm on my way to Halifax with my brother-in-law Don. Since our previous trip to the New England States had gone so smoothly, I have volunteered to join him again, this time on a trip to pick up a boat.

The *Marian Antonia* is a sturdy vessel, built to withstand her previous rugged life as a Newfoundland coastal freighter. New owners had hired Don to deliver her to Barbados.

The passage from Newfoundland to Nova Scotia had been a rough one. Carrying a crew of three—Don, my father Raymond, and my sister Rikki—the *Marian Antonia* left St. Pierre under sunny skies, and a few short hours later, sailed straight into the teeth of a vicious Atlantic storm. Twenty-four hours after leaving port, she staggered into Canso with a hold half-full of water; battered and beaten, but still afloat.

Unfortunately, the *Thomas E Hodder*, a wooden schooner that had left around the same time, taking the same route, was not so lucky. It went down in the Gulf of St. Lawrence during the storm, resulting in five lives lost. There was only one survivor.

## Ben Robicheau

There was now no doubt the *Marian Antonia* could withstand rough weather, but the trip had uncovered a few shortcomings. An electrical problem was preventing the batteries from charging, one of the two diesel engines was either leaking or burning an unusual amount of motor oil, and the boat was not equipped with radar or any sort of ship-to-shore communications. In fact, the only piece of modern electrical equipment she did have installed was a depth sounder, and that wasn't working.

The owners had arranged for the boat to be left in Halifax for a couple of weeks, where it would be gone over, stem to stern and these deficiencies could be resolved. This work was scheduled to be completed by now, so Don and I were on our way to bring her home to Brier Island. Our plan was to sail the newly-renovated vessel non-stop, arriving in Westport on the day before Christmas Eve.

Sometimes plans just don't work out. Due to some dispute or misunderstanding that we had not been made aware of, nothing at all had been done, and now the shipyard was shutting down for the holidays. Since Don's contract stipulated that the boat be delivered to Barbados by a certain date, we had no choice but to fix up what we could, the best we could, ourselves.

There was nothing we could do about the lack of radar and ship-to-shore, but we did get the depth sounder working. The electrical problem turned out to be the result of old, tired batteries, which we replaced. The oil consumption problem on the one en-

## Two Ferries Out

gine was internal, and far beyond our abilities to fix in the time we had available, so we took care of that problem by laying in a case of motor oil.

We managed to get things ship-shape enough that we were able to cast off from the Halifax waterfront about mid-morning on the 23rd. We were leaving a day later than planned, with the intention of sailing straight through the night. With fair winds and some luck, we should still be able to make it home in plenty of time to celebrate Christmas Eve with the family.

Again, plans don't always work out. By late afternoon, we found ourselves struggling along in a blinding snowstorm. Since we had no radar, we navigated by following the barely-visible shoreline, but as it became harder and harder to see, in the falling darkness, Don decided it was best to put in for the night. The next day was Christmas Eve day. If the weather was good when we woke up, we'd continue on. If not, we'd call for someone to come pick us up, and just leave the boat where it was until after Christmas.

The next morning dawned clear and sunny. It looked like we were going to be able to make it home for Christmas Eve after all.

By mid-afternoon, we were approaching the southern end of the province. We would soon be rounding the tip and heading back up St. Mary's Bay.

As we ventured on, the wind started to pick up, and the dark clouds began spitting snow. Conditions continued to intensify until we found ourselves being tossed about by high winds and waves, and completely enshrouded in thick, wet, horizontally blowing snow, bringing visibility down to almost zero.

Our charts showed that we were now in an area dotted with small islands, so to be safe we reduced speed and kept a close watch for reefs and rocks—not easy to do when visibility ended just beyond the bow. Just as my eyes were feeling like they were about to fall out of their sockets from the strain, I made out the faint outline of an island.

We knew that some of these islands are inhabited for part of the year. If this was one of the islands that had a house on it, then it would also have a wharf. If it had a wharf, that might be a place for us to tie up and wait out the storm.

We circled the island, both of us staring intently at the shoreline, hoping for a small cove or some sort of suitable sheltering place. Something made me lift my eyes away from the hazy shoreline and look towards the bow. Directly ahead, I saw the surf breaking over a huge boulder.

I yelled. Don instantly reacted by spinning the wheel as far over as it would go, and simultaneously throwing the engines into full reverse; we both braced for the strike.

After what seemed an agonizing eternity, the forward motion of the *Marian Antonia* ceased and she slowly began to reverse. We missed the rock by what must have been mere inches, but in the process, had got turned around, and lost sight of the island in the thickening snow. We were now completely disoriented. We had charts and a compass, but with no visible landmarks, they were pretty much useless to us.

By now, darkness was encroaching. We were even further blinded as the snow thickened, and on every side were unseen islands and ledges. We had to keep moving to avoid drifting and being battered by waves, but had no way of knowing which was a safe direction.

Don decided our only option was to set a straight course, follow it until the depth sounder indicated we were nearing dangerously shallow water, then turn around and run the same course back again.

For the next few hours we took turns at the wheel, following the compass back and forth, surrounded by invisible islands, being tossed about by wind and waves, nearly hypnotized by the snow whipping across the deck in a mesmerizingly sinuous, continuous stream, glowing pure white under the glaring deck lights.

Every hour or so, we had to add more oil to the starboard engine. Our supply was rapidly running low. The wheelhouse floor became covered in spilled oil, tracked up from the engine room; it was like standing on a sheet of ice. Whoever was at the wheel had to maintain a tight grip to keep from sliding clear across the wheelhouse every time the boat rolled or nosed up and down over a wave.

With two diesel engines running continuously, we were burning through a lot of fuel. By ten P.M., the gauge indicated our tanks were nearly empty. Fortunately, we had spare fuel. Unfortunately, this meant we had to venture out on deck with a length of rubber hose to siphon the diesel from the oil drums lashed to the mast, into the below-deck tanks.

After half an hour of wrestling oil drums around a heaving, slush-covered deck while being pelted by salt spray, soaked by wet, sticky snow, and after the decidedly unpleasant experience of sucking a mouthful of diesel through the siphon hose, we managed to get the tanks refilled.

A couple of hours later, I was at the wheel, burping up diesel fumes, when I noticed the snow seemed to be thinning. Suddenly I caught a flash of light off in the distance. A lighthouse!

I shouted to Don, and by the time he got the charts out, I had spotted a second light. Two lights enabled us to triangulate and figure out where we were, and with visibility now rapidly improving, we were able to finally set a course for home.

As we entered St. Mary's Bay, we had to shut down our problematic engine, as we had finally used up the last of our motor oil. Running at reduced speed, we were taking on a lot of spray, and by the time we passed Peter's Island just before dawn, the *Marian Antonia* must have looked a sorry sight, limping along on one engine, covered in frozen salt spray, and with a severe list due to the weight of several inches of ice she was now carrying on the windward side.

As we approached the wharf, I was surprised to see Dick Thompson standing ready to catch our lines. It struck me as a bit odd that he would be there at five a.m. on Christmas morning. I found out later that he had been up all night, driving back and forth from Southern Point to Western Light, one of several people on the island who had spent the night watching for any sign of our approach.

Dick dropped us off at my parent's house, just as the eastern sky began to lighten. We tried to enter quietly so as to not wake anyone, but were barely inside the kitchen door when the lights came on, and we heard Dad say, "I'm some glad to see you boys."

Within seconds, everyone in the house was up, and the kitchen was filled with a lot of hugging, talking and some relieved crying.

It hadn't occurred to me until that second, that anyone would be worried about us. But it turned out that Dick Thompson was not the only one who had had a sleepless night.

### Rikki's experience

It was Christmas Eve 1969, my first Christmas as a married woman. My husband and brother were on their way home to Westport from Halifax, by boat, in a snowstorm.

My Dad, my husband Don, and I had brought the boat, the *Marian Antonia*, to Halifax from Marystown, Newfoundland. We would be delivering it after Christmas to Barbados for Bellaire Institute of Oceanography, part of McGill University, to be used as a floating laboratory there. Don was the captain; my Dad, first mate; and I was the cook.

**Ben Robicheau**

We had left Newfoundland at the end of November, and then spent a week on the French colony of Saint Pierre, waiting for the weather to clear.

After getting the all-clear from the coast guard, we set off for Canso. That night we ended up in a terrible storm. Our boat was not equipped with radar or radio telephone, so we could not send or receive any distress signals. We were to find out later that a boat with five men aboard, crossing very close to where we were, had not been as lucky as we were!

We made it to Halifax on December 7th, my 19th birthday, and left the boat there to be refitted for the next part of the trip. The refit was supposed to have happened before we left Newfoundland.

Dad was needed at home right away because of the busy Christmas season in the store, and I was helping out at home, so Ben now filled in for the trip from Halifax to Brier Island. But winter was coming and, as we had found out earlier, the Gulf of Saint Lawrence and the North Atlantic could be unpredictable at this time of year.

At home, the weather on Christmas Eve was stormy, and there was no sign of them yet! The wind had picked up and it was like a blizzard out on the water.

As I stood staring out the bedroom window, long past the expected arrival time, looking for any sign of a light, or sound of a boat, a dreadful feeling came over me. Oh my God, what if they never arrive? Other boats had gone down in these conditions and on that same route.

## Two Ferries Out

Also, I had a little secret I hadn't shared with the family yet. Now it was possible I was not only going to be a widow and lose my brother, but I was going to be a single mother.

All night, we got reports from the locals who were keeping a look-out,. One in particular, Dick Thompson, watched from Southern Point.

Finally, by three or four in the morning, I had cried myself to sleep, exhausted and dreading the worst.

Then, just at daybreak, there was a commotion down in the kitchen. It was my Dad's voice. He was talking to someone. Do I dare get up and receive the terrible news?

Then I heard Mom calling me.

There they stood, half frozen and reeking of diesel fuel. The best sight and Christmas present ever.

I guess I learned the true meaning of Christmas that year!

**Ben Robicheau**

*Low fog over Westport.*

## 36: Fogged in

I always looked forward to the arrival of September on the Island. You start to feel a bit of a nip in the air, and though sad to see another summer go, it's often a relief to finally leave the fog season behind, and be able to enjoy the sometimes brilliantly clear, fresh days of early Fall.

As a kid, I thought that the quality and quantity of fog we experienced, sometimes on a daily basis, was unique to the Islands. But as an adult, I lived for a summer in Louisburg, Cape Breton. I now know that there is at least one other place that can equal us for the density of its summer air.

One of the things that always amazed me about fog was how many different types there are. I've often thought that we should be like the Inuit, who have many different names for snow, depending on the quality of it.

It was sometimes easy to forget that the whole world wasn't living in a thick, cold, wet cloud. In my childhood days, people didn't leave the Island as frequently as they do today. I remember going up through Long Island after several weeks of being socked in at Westport. By the time we reached Lily Small's place in Central Grove, the fog was thinning and I was amazed and startled to glimpse the sun. I had forgotten that not everyone was spending their summer living under an unrelenting wet, grey blanket.

Of course, as we approached Tiverton, the fog was hovering once more over the cold waters of Petite Passage, and we again had to drive with our headlights on. Once we got on the mainland, it would usually be clear sailing up The Neck, except for brief dips back into the soup when we came near the water at Little River, Sandy Cove and Seawall Hill.

In those days, clothes dryers were still not a common item in most households, so every backyard had a clothesline. Because of the fog, it was not unusual to see the same clothes on the line for several days in a row, still trying to get dry.

My mother did the laundry for our large family, usually with one, and sometimes two, kids in cloth diapers, and trying to get things dry on a line was often a frustrating ordeal. If the fog was in solid, nothing dried at all. In fact, the clothes usually got wetter than when they came from the wringer. If the fog did clear out, you had to keep a sharp eye and time it just right, to bring the laundry in again before the fog rolled back in, or any drying achieved during the brief period of sun would be lost.

Sometimes the fog would drift leisurely in and out several times in a day, alternately wetting and drying any washing on the line. Many times, Mom was forced to concede defeat to the whims of the fog, and had to string up her laundry in the porch, or across the kitchen.

## Two Ferries Out

The fog would sometimes burn off over the land, but would still linger over the colder water. This made for some interesting situations for a fog-watcher. I remember seeing the fog densely covering the harbour from the water surface up to a height of three or four feet, with nothing but clear, brilliant sun above. A boat would go by, and all you could see would be the cabin and spars moving along above a grey mist. At other times, weather conditions would cause the fog to reverse itself and hover a few feet above the water. In this case, you could clearly see the hull of a boat going by with the upper part hidden from view.

Some days, the fog would move aside like a curtain, granting us a few hours of sunshine over the Islands and Passages, but hovering just offshore, a dense grey wall, ready to sweep back in at a moment's notice, a constant reminder not to get too used to that rare commodity, sunshine!

In the mid-sixties, when the Digby scallop fleet was fishing out of Westport, they had a reputation for being, shall we say, economical, and only one boat in the whole fleet had radar. On foggy days, the boats all stayed at the wharf until that one radar-equipped boat left, then they all followed her out. When the skipper decided to come back in, they all followed him in. If he decided to return to Digby a day early, the whole fleet left a day early. Without radar or the intimate knowledge of the area that local fishermen had, the fog made the whole Digby scallop fleet helpless.

**Ben Robicheau**

For us teenagers living on the Island, fog was a major factor in our lives. We used to listen mostly to radio station WMEX from Boston because they had disc jockey Arnie (Woo Woo) Ginsburg with all the late-breaking news on those new bands from England (the Beatles, the Rolling Stones) and all the other important things we wanted to know about. Interspersed with the music, they had weather reports, and it always seemed that, if they were reporting very hot weather in Boston, we could be assured of thick fog the next day.

We didn't let bad weather stop our teen-age social activities. We did the things we always did, but wiener roasts in Pond Cove were not quite as much fun with banks of cold wet fog rolling in off the sea to the not-so-melodic accompaniment of the Western Light foghorn moaning in the background.

Riding our bicycles or, when we got older, motorcycles in the fog was not much fun, either, especially in the evening when the fog seemed to take on an even denser, heavier quality. Besides the difficulty it added to seeing where you were going after dark, after a few minutes in the saddle, you were usually freezing cold and dripping wet. Also, the fog collected in puddles and made the grass wet and slippery, so it was dangerous to zip through people's backyards and between houses playing one of our favourite games, "bicycle tag".

Another social event the fog affected was the weekly Saturday-night dance at Lloyd's Hall in Freeport. In those days, the ferry stopped running at dusk but would make special trips after dark, if the weather was good. Sometimes, you didn't even get to the dance, either because the fog was too thick for the ferry to make the trip in the first place, or because you knew it was going to get that thick later on, and you stood a good chance of not being able to get back. The dance ended at midnight, and the ferry would usually arrive to pick up the returning dance-goers at quarter after twelve. Many times, long before Fats Domino sang, "I Want to Walk You Home", signalling the last dance of the night, a rumour would sweep the Hall that the fog was coming in and the ferry was making its last trip early. Most of the Westporters would have to cut their evening short and head for Fish Point.

Sometimes the fog came in so suddenly that everyone would be stranded. Some lucky people found accommodations with friends. The unlucky ones walked the foggy roads until morning light, or maybe spent the night cramped and shivering in their cars.

Even though it can sometimes be depressing, and after eight straight days or so of constant cold and damp you might think that you've seen enough fog to last a lifetime, I have to admit that it can sometimes also be spectacularly beautiful. Lifting over the Passage with the brilliant sun glaring off it, or hanging in the harbour entrance like a great grey brooding giant, the fog is an impressive, and in some ways unique, force of nature that we might not always appreciate.

**Ben Robicheau**

My sister Virginia owns Brier Island Lodge. When she went into the hotel business, one of her first guests was a gentleman from the U.S. who booked one night in order to go whale watching. The next morning brought thick fog, and whale watching was cancelled for the day, so he booked to stay another night, and spent the day walking the Island, returning soaked from the mist and the wet grass in the fields.

The next morning the harbour was socked in again, no trip out, so he stayed one more night, and did more walking in the fog. When the third day was still foggy, Virginia, thinking he must be getting bored with all the fog and endless walking, told him the forecast said it might be two or three more days before a shift in the wind would move the fog out, so maybe he might want to go somewhere else that could offer a bit more in the way of sunshine.

With a chuckle, he told her that he was from Arizona, and after a lifetime of hot, dry weather, he thought the fog was wonderful, fascinating and refreshing! He stayed several more days, just to enjoy the fog.

## 37: Hurricane season

August, 2005, dramatically reminded the world of the devastating power of the hurricane when Katrina nearly wiped out the city of New Orleans. Since then, news sources intently track and breathlessly report on any tropical storm that develops. The networks seem to think that they have discovered some new and unique phenomenon.

Here on the islands, we are well acquainted with the storms that arrive every Fall with unfailing regularity. One of the first officially-recorded hurricanes in this area was the 1869 Saxby Gale, which struck the Bay of Fundy region during a Saros tide, an unusually-high tide that occurs once every eighteen years. This unfortunate combination caused severe flooding in New Brunswick and Nova Scotia. In August of 1873, Eastern Canada was hit with what was probably its worst storm in recorded history. What became known as The Nova Scotia Hurricane left over 600 people dead and destroyed more than 1,200 boats and 900 buildings. It was the first storm for which an official hurricane warning was issued.

In 2003, we experienced Hurricane Juan, which missed most of this end of the province but hit Halifax hard, causing over three hundred million dollars in damage and taking the lives of eight people. Juan is considered to be the worst storm to hit Halifax since 1893. Because of the havoc Juan wreaked, the Meteorological Service of Canada officially retired the name from use.

Closer to home, our own worst storm of the century would have to be the Groundhog Day Storm of 1976, which, like The Saxby Gale, arrived on a Saros tide. Although classified as a winter storm, it carried sustained winds of 164km/hr, making it equal to a Category 2 hurricane. It struck an unprepared coastline almost without warning, and did tens of millions of dollars in damage to roadways, utilities, buildings and fishing equipment in the south-west area of the Province. We are lucky that storms of such destructive calibre are not the norm.

Still, even a small hurricane is not something to take lightly. Even as a child, I became aware of a tension in the air as we got towards the end of August. This was due to the uncertainty that the fishermen, and anyone who had property on the waterfront, began to feel as we got into that time of year when things started brewing in the southern oceans. It was only a matter of time, before one of those storms would come knocking on our door. The big question was; how hard would it knock?

When we heard of a storm heading our way, fishermen would begin making preparations. The expected fierceness of the storm, the direction it was coming from, and what the tide level would be when it hit were all factors to take into consideration. If wind speeds were not too high and the tide was expected to be low during the worst of the storm, some might

## Two Ferries Out

take a chance on grounding their boat out beside their wharf at the high-water mark, or maybe even just letting it ride out the storm on the moorings.

If it looked like things might get dirty, some fishermen would avoid the possibility of boat damage from banging up against wharves or grounding out on the beach by taking their boats out into the middle of the harbour and riding out the worst of the storm there. Other boats might be tied up on the protected lee side of the breakwater, or hauled right out onto dry land. If we expected even more ferocious winds, tide and wind direction were in their favour, they could make for the safety of the Freeport cove, or head across St. Mary's Bay to the shelter of the Meteghan wharf. They might even go inland, up the Sissaboo River at Weymouth. In Tiverton, if the tide was right and you could get in under the bridge, there was room to tie up a few boats in the pond.

Ashore, things would be getting busy, too. We hauled punts up off the beach, stowed away or lashed down gear on wharves, and secured extra lines and bumpers on boats that were going to ride it out at the wharf.

We also took precautions at home. We checked flashlight batteries, filled oil lamps, and counted candles, ready for the inevitable power outage: and if your house was on the Front Road, you might want to board up your windows.

Then, after all that preparation and worry, we would usually have one of the nicest days of the summer. The air being pushed in front of the hurricane often brought a blazing sun in a cloudless sky, and weather that was muggy and hot and deadly still. Although this was a nice break from the usual Island weather of fog or cold ocean wind, it had an ominous feeling about it, and it usually only lasted a few hours.

The first indication you got that things were about to turn nasty was when you realized that the dead calm had given way to a light breeze. This gentle wind would steadily increase in intensity until, almost before you knew it, you found yourself fighting to stay on your feet while horizontal sheets of rain pelted you.

Okay, now we were getting down to it. This thing that the fishermen on the wharves, the old men on the store bench, and the kids at school had been talking about for the last few days, was finally here.

Being a kid, and not fully realizing the full destructive potential of a storm like this, I enjoyed the wildness and ferocity that a hurricane brought with it, and saw it as nothing more than a time of excitement and adventure. Everyone was on high alert, the village actually seemed busier than on a normal day, men were out on the streets and wharves in their oilskins and rubber boots, shouting back and forth over the howling wind while constantly checking boat lines and keeping a sharp eye out for signs that some supporting wharf timber or post might be starting to weaken under the relentless pounding of the waves.

Suddenly, there would be a sudden burst of action. Someone's boat has broken free from its moorings and is drifting towards the rocks, or a drifting log has gotten loose in the rolling waves and is smashing the poles out from under someone's wharf! Then, you might see someone risking his life to jump onto the rain-slicked, heaving deck of a boat that was beating itself to pieces against a wharf, or two men working together to lasso and tie off a piece of floating debris before it could do further damage.

Back at home, mothers were now busy trying to keep their children away from the windows and distracted from the howling noise outside. Our house was right across the road from the beach and would often be lashed with salt spray during storms, During one particularly vicious storm that had already knocked out the power, a beach rock came flying through our living-room window. My sisters and I spent the next several hours huddled around a candle in the bathroom, sitting on sofa cushions, listening to my mother trying to distract us by telling stories and singing songs.

Dramatic instances like this were, I am glad to say, not the norm. With most storms, it was usually just a long night of wind and rain, and the occasional dramatic spray of salt water over the road. If the eye of the storm happened to pass directly overhead, the wind would diminish at some point and the sun or stars would appear for a short time in a clear, cloudless sky; then the wind would start again, but from the opposite direction this time as the back half of the storm passed over us.

After it was all over, there would be cleaning up to do. Even if it was what I saw as a disappointingly meek hurricane, there would still be the odd section of missing breastwork, maybe a few yards of washed-out roadway, boards missing on a few wharves and a neat little shoal of beach gravel and sand in someone's front yard where the waves had washed across the Front Road. Up at The Dike you would probably see two things: the road covered with flat stones from the near-by beach, and the Nova Scotia Power crew trying to get the power back on. The underwater cable that carries the electricity to the Island comes ashore here, and it seems that the flying salt spray from almost every storm, big or small, manages to short out the transformers and burn off the connectors.

Whenever the power went out, I would hope that it would take several days to restore. As soon as the lights went off, Dad would head to his store and lock up the ice cream freezer, cover it with blankets for insulation, and put pop cases on the lids to keep them closed tight to hold the cold in. This would keep the contents frozen for about three or four days. Any longer than that, and it was most likely a lost cause, and there would be nothing left to do but eat the ice cream before it all totally melted. I was always more than willing to do my part to see that it didn't go to waste.

**Two Ferries Out**

Although they could be very destructive and the cause of a lot of worry for the fishermen of the Island, for some of us little kids hurricanes provided an exciting break from the ordinary, day-to-day Island life...and, sometimes, free ice cream.

## Ben Robicheau

*Rough weather.*

## 38: Smoke on the water

In addition to hurricane season, another exciting time of the year was grass burning season. You could usually detect the arrival of this traditional sign of spring on Brier Island by simply opening a window or stepping out onto your doorstep. There you might very well notice an unmistakable, smoky-wet-wood smell drifting over the island: someone, somewhere had a grass fire going.

The springtime ritual of burning off dead winter grass has probably been carried on since humans first discovered fire, and some of the original reasons for doing so, are still in practice today. Those who have grazing animals will burn off last year's dead grass so the new, green shoots can show through and give their horses, cows or sheep a break from that dusty, dry, winter hay. Others do it for appearance; the easiest way to get rid of all of that unsightly, matted, dead grass lining the edge of the yard or wrapped around the lower strands of a wire fence is to just put a match to it. Still others have safety in mind. Having fields of tinder-dry grass around your house and buildings during the summer months is not a good idea. The results of a carelessly-tossed cigarette could be catastrophic; a controlled burn gets rid of that potential problem.

Unfortunately, even though people may start grass fires with the best of intentions, that first scent of smoke is often followed in short order by the sound of sirens as the local fire department rushes to a blaze that has spread out of control.

One spring a gentleman of the town, who shall remain nameless, decided to get rid of some burdock bushes in his backyard. After dousing them with kerosene and setting them alight, he decided to step inside the house for a few minutes. Not surprisingly, this turned out to be a bad idea.

Upon his return, he was astounded to see that his little burdock fire had grown impressively in size, spread to a nearby field, and was now racing before a brisk wind through the long grass behind the houses of the village. Luckily, the breeze was pushing the fire away from the houses and along through the fields that lie between the hill and the village.

In short order, most of the Island men were heading for the fields armed with shovels, rakes, wet burlap bags, and any other make-shift fire-fighting tools that they could quickly grab, in the hopes of stopping the fire in its tracks or, at the very least, preventing it from doing serious damage. By the time they reached the front edge of the fire, it was moving along at a rapid clip, pushing a wall of flames that reached to a height of fifteen or twenty feet in some places.

One of the first casualties of this inferno was a camp halfway up Joe's Hill that teenagers Braddie and Everett Titus had built out of scavenged lumber.

## Two Ferries Out

All their hard work was reduced to smouldering ash in an instant.

The flames then sped along towards Edgar McDormand's big building in the field behind his house. Luckily, Edgar was the type of man who liked to keep his properties looking good, so the mowed grass around this structure formed a protective green area that slowed down the fire enough to allow the fire fighters to fend off the flames.

This event took place before there was any sort of organized fire department on the island, and it was soon obvious that, without proper equipment, the only real hope the fire fighters had was that the blaze would burn itself out before it did any real damage. Daniel's Road lay right across the fire's path. If they could hold the fire there, it might starve itself out.

The firefighters massed along the narrow road, some still in the barvels and rubber gloves they had been wearing as they ran from the fishplants.

Despite their valiant attempt to contain the flames, a few sparks managed to leap this barrier and spread rapidly into the knee-high grass field across the road. Just as the fire was getting a good hold, the wind suddenly shifted, blowing directly towards the village.

The first building in its path was the old Coggins house, which was now home for several of the very fishplant workers who were fighting to put out the fire. The long field grass grew right up to the back wall and, to make matters worse, there was a pile of firewood only a few feet from the house. The flames were shooting high into the air and speeding down the field at a rate the men were unable to match. It looked like the house was gone for sure.

Then, at the very last second, with the flames just short of the woodpile, the wind shifted once again. It was coming now from the exact opposite direction, it blew the fire back on itself and the flames, starved of new fuel, dropped to a level at which the shovels and burlap bags could be effective.

Although this offshoot of the fire was defeated, the main body carried on, finally exhausting itself just before reaching the High Knoll. But it went out with one last destructive gasp, sending a camp that Chester and Harry Lent had built at the base of the hill behind their house up in flames. Ironically, once the last of the wildfire embers had been extinguished, it was discovered that the burdock bushes that had instigated this fiasco had survived with only minor scorching.

Of course, not every fire resulted in near-disaster. Night-time skating parties on Lively's Pond often involved a roaring bonfire that provided a chance to warm up a bit, and enough flickering light to let you see some of the thin ice and soft spots at the edge of the pond. Bonfires were also popular in the summer months; on many an evening at Pond Cove, we would roast hot dogs and marshmallows over a roaring driftwood fire while everyone huddled up as close to the warmth of the flames as possible. The wind baffling across the beach usually kept you busy ducking sparks and eye-watering smoke, while allowing you to experience that unique bilateral sensation of feeling like the front of your body was about to burst into flames at the very same time that your back was freezing and wet from the fog drifting in off the ocean.

You could cook things other than the traditional hot dog on a beach fire. If you got hungry while hiking the back shore, you could use a little fire inside a circle of stones to boil up some periwinkles in a tin can scavenged off the beach. If you didn't happen to have a pin to pick the meat out of the shells, a nail pulled from one of the nearby, busted-up lobster traps would do just fine.

One of the most innovative ways of cooking on a beach fire that I can remember, occurred during a family picnic at Scataway Cove. We started a large fire, and while it was burning we collected some mussels. Since we hadn't brought any pots, I wasn't sure what we were going to do with the mussels, but I soon found out.

When the fire had burned down to white-hot embers, my father came up the beach with an armload of wet seaweed, which he threw down on the coals. As the fire sizzled and popped, he put the mussels on top of the seaweed and covered them with more seaweed. After a few minutes he pulled the top layer back to reveal some nicely-steamed mussels.

Of course, not every fire has to have a function or a purpose. Some are just for fun, and for a kid, the Back Shore is ideal for this. There are usually no adults around, the beach is littered with combustible material, and it is a relatively safe place to build a fire. What kid who just happens to have left home with a couple of matches in his pocket could resist?

Most of the fires we built were simple bonfires, set far enough down the beach that there was no danger of catching the grass and trees ablaze. And after we got tired of the fire, we had the fun of watching it die hissing and spitting in the rising tide. Occasionally, we would give an old wooden lobster crate a Viking funeral by lashing it to a couple of sticks of pulp wood, then setting it adrift and afire on the ocean.

One summer, a couple of friends and I discovered a large propane tank washed ashore not far from Copper Mine Cove. In the past, we had enjoyed the pyrotechnics caused by blowing up old aerosol cans, so we felt this was an opportunity not to be missed. After building a huge fire on the beach, we picked up the tank, swung it back and forth between us, and pitched it into the middle of the fire. We could hear some remaining gas sloshing around in the tank, so we knew the fireworks were going to be good. We ran up into the field and ducked down behind a little hill, peeking over the top and waiting expectantly for the big bang.

We waited…and waited…but nothing happened. We finally decided that the tank must be a dud, full of water instead of gas, and were just starting down the hill to investigate, when there was a terrific explosion. We all hit the ground as bits and pieces of flaming debris rained down around us. We looked up to see dozens of little grass fires radiating out from the smoking crater where our fire had been.

After fifteen minutes of running around frantically stomping and swatting, we managed to put out all the fires, although in the process one of our group ruined his new jacket by using it to beat out the flames.

Just before we hit the ground, I had noticed a hiker coming over a rise on the trail along the shore, not far from the fire. When I looked up after the explosion, I caught a glimpse of him heading back the way he had come, but at a much brisker pace. His peaceful walk with nature had turned into something more like a hike through a war zone!

I might be many years too late with this, but whoever that hiker was, I'm sorry for almost blowing you up!

# Ben Robicheau

## 39: Rock music

Anyone lucky enough to spend even a brief period of time at the end of Digby Neck soon becomes acutely aware that the Islands produce their own distinctive brand of music, a kind of natural "rock music" generated by the constant wave action. This rocky repertoire ranges from the almost-subliminal heavy bass sound of boulders thumping together as they are shoved around the harbour bottom during a fierce winter storm, to the high-pitched tinkling cadence of pebbles being dragged up and down the beach by gently lapping waves on a fine summer's day.

Some visitors find these sounds musical and soothing; some others might be annoyed by the constant, but always changing, noise. For those who live here, the familiar sounds of the Island sometimes recede into the background; somewhere in our brains we are still aware of them, but don't really tune into them unless something brings them to the front of the mind.

This background music came to my full attention with a vengeance one foggy fall evening when I was nine years old. I had stayed longer than usual at my father's store and was walking home by myself in the dark. As I made my way along the sparsely-lit Front Road, I became gradually aware of the noises rising from the beach. The most obvious of these was a sort of rhythmic rustling sound, beneath which I could detect a heavy, muted, clunking and a variety of higher-pitched rattling noises, accentuated by a sort of metallic scraping sound.

These sounds were not strange to me. I had been hearing them all my life, and I knew perfectly well that it was just the action of the waves moving a few of the bigger rocks around and, in those bad old days before garbage collection, washing some old bottles and tin cans up and down the beach. But as I walked along alone through the dark, semi-preoccupied with trying to avoid stepping in mud puddles, my mind took this opportunity to play tricks on me. In the otherwise-quiet darkness, the familiar sounds emanating from out of the mist seemed to be getting louder and louder, and my nine-year-old imagination began to produce alternative and infinitely more interesting possibilities for the sources of those noises.

Now that I had become hyper-aware of it, the eerie rustling/clunking didn't sound like waves at all; in fact, it more closely resembled the sound a huge sea creature might make while slithering its way up the beach. And that rattling noise might not be caused by bottles, but by the monster's cruel and vicious yellow claws scrabbling on the rocks. Then there was that ominous metallic scraping sound, clearly the result of horrible giant scales dragging over the rocks as it steadily made its way up the beach on its way to hunt me down.

At this point, I thought it prudent to move over to the other side of the road to have as much space as possible between us when this terrible sea-dragon finally reared its ugly head over the breastwork to glare at me with fiery, blood-shot eyes.

By now, the possibility of stepping in a puddle was the least of my worries; I walked as fast as I could along the far edge of the road, looking straight ahead and carefully avoiding even a glance towards the beach, working on the somewhat dubious theory that if I didn't see *him*, then he wouldn't be able to see *me*.

When I finally arrived, out of breath but safe, on my doorstep, it was with a small feeling of relief, and a much larger feeling of sheepishness for letting my imagination run away with me. I was nine years old, after all, too old to believe in dragons and sea creatures! Still, for the next little while, any time I had to walk the roads by myself after dark, I studiously avoided the Front Road.

It wasn't only the waves that added to the Island soundscape. On many a foggy summer's evening we would be serenaded by the constant trumpeting of the foghorns. Unlike the whiny electronic foghorns of today, the old, air-powered analog horns almost talked to you, not in an annoyingly robotic wail, but in a deep resounding voice. You could actually hear them breathe in and out as the compressed air passed through. If you happened to be standing close enough when they spoke, you could sometimes feel the sound waves vibrate through your body.

Another distinctive sound along the waterfront in those days was that of boat engines. In the fifties and sixties there were more boats than today, and the harbour would resonate almost constantly with the sound of boats coming and going. Most of the local fishing boats were much smaller than those in use today, and were powered by old car engines. We kids were so used to the comings and goings of these boats that we could identify which boat it was without even looking, just by the sound of its engine.

You would think that one old car engine would sound more or less like the next old car engine, but each boat had its own distinctive sound, probably because people were very inventive with their exhaust systems. Some boats had no mufflers at all, some had store-bought mufflers, and some had home-made mufflers fashioned from water pressure tanks, metal floaters, propane cylinders...just about anything that was hollow and could withstand the ravages of the salt air better than a regular car muffler or even the marine mufflers that were available.

Every time I visit the Islands these days, I hear some familiar sounds that probably haven't changed in a million years and will most likely still be there a million years from now. Then there are other sounds that I listen for in vain, sounds that existed only for a brief period. Their day has now passed, leaving us only with the long-ago memory of voices we will never hear again.

## 40: On the road with Murf the Surf

As I got older, more of my life experiences took place off the Island; but surprisingly, in many cases they still retained some connection, however tenuous, to Brier Island. In the Spring of 1968 an opportunity for a bit of off-island adventure arose when I received a letter from my friend Jonathon Ross in Florida. Jonathon's mother was originally from Nova Scotia and, every couple of years, Mary, her husband Ernie, and their family would travel from their home in Hawaii to spend the summer at the family home near Digby. Jonathon spent quite a bit of time on Brier Island and, because of where he was from, the local kids of course had to label him "Murf the Surf".

The Rosses had arrived in Nova Scotia the previous summer, but because Ernie was on sabbatical from his job at the University of Hawaii, they didn't go back home when the summer was over. Instead, they headed south to Gainesville, Florida, where Ernie was doing research at the University of Florida. Jonathon soon found himself an after-school job, and used his earnings to buy a motorcycle.

When spring arrived and Mary and Ernie began planning their return to N.S., Jonathon thought it would be fun to make the trip north on his bike. Although far from thrilled, his parents agreed to let him go, on the condition that he find someone to go with him. A few days later I got the letter.

Jonathon's plan was that I would arrive in Florida just as he was finishing his school year, and we would return to N.S. together. I thought that was a great idea.

The previous summer I had bought a second-hand motorcycle; actually, it was more like third-or-fourth hand, a 1960 Honda that had seen better days. On my way to catch the Yarmouth ferry to Bar Harbor, Maine, it started leaking oil, and a mechanic discovered that a gasket needed replacing. When I told him that I was setting out on my way to Florida, the whole shop had a good laugh. They told me in no uncertain terms that this old junker would never make it.

With a new gasket installed and those less-than-encouraging words ringing in my ears, I made my way to the ferry.

On the long trip across the Bay, I passed the time by talking with the man in the next seat, who, it turned out, was on his way home to Bangor after attending a church event in Nova Scotia. As we neared the Maine coast, the sky darkened, and it began to rain. Before we parted, my new-found friend handed me his address and told me that if I didn't want to ride in this weather, he and his family could put me up.

I hoped that once I got inland, things would improve, but a half hour later the rain was coming down in sheets, I was soaked and cold, and even

## Two Ferries Out

though the address he had given me was well out of my way, the offer of shelter for the night started looking pretty good.

When I arrived in Bangor, they welcomed me with a hot meal and the opportunity to dry my clothes. Warm and fed, I was just getting ready to settle in for the evening when my host informed me that we were off to a Christian revival meeting.

This meeting took place in a huge high-school auditorium, with what looked like several thousand people in attendance. It was very impressive for someone coming from Islands Consolidated, where our school's combination gym/assembly hall/lunchroom would be hard-pressed to seat much more than two or three hundred.

The program involved performances by the school ROTC drill team, which consisted of impressive and precise military drills, marching back and forth while spinning and twirling rifles. It seemed a bit odd to me, it being a religious meeting and all, but everyone else seemed to enjoy it.

The main speaker of the evening was Paul Anderson, an Olympic weightlifter who at one point had held the title of strongest man in the world. He spoke about how his religion helped him to overcome the effects of the flu and go on to win a gold medal over a Russian competitor at the Olympics in Australia. He finished off his speech by lifting up a wooden platform with several football players and the cheerleading squad on it.

**Ben Robicheau**

At six the next morning, my host asked me to help set up tables and chairs for a weekly breakfast meeting at his church. The rain had stopped overnight, and it looked like it was going to be a nice day. I was eager to get on my way and make up for lost time, but the offer of free food was just too hard to pass up, so I packed up my bike and followed him to the church.

It turned out that the weightlifter from the night before was a special guest at this gathering. After a bit of light labour involving the tables and chairs, I got to enjoy a very good breakfast and have a nice chat with Mr. Anderson, who was interested in my trip, and also in motorcycles. He said he used to have a Harley he rode around his farm in Georgia, but it eventually fell apart under his weight. He weighed about 360 pounds, all of it muscle, and had at one time set a world record by lifting more than 1200 pounds.

By eight a.m. all the breakfasters were off to work, the world's strongest man wished me safe journey, and I was finally on the road and headed south.

I had packed a tent, and my plan was to camp out along the way. Just before dark I would pull off the main road onto a likely-looking side road, find a field full of corn or some other tall crop, drive my bike around the perimeter of the field until I was out of sight, and then set up my tent. I felt relatively safe doing this, as no one could see me and nobody knew I was there.

## Two Ferries Out

By the time I got to the State of Georgia, I felt pretty secure with this system. I bunked down for the night at the back of a field next to a grove of old, moss-covered trees. At some time during the night, I was startled awake by the sound of a loud roaring and thrashing going on somewhere in the woods. I lay awake listening for a while. It wasn't too far away, but didn't seem to be getting any closer, and eventually it died out, so I went back to sleep.

The next morning, as I got back out on the main road, I noticed a large sign reading, "Warning! You are entering The Okefenokee Swamp. Please stay in your car, and beware of alligators."

I had camped on the edge of an alligator sanctuary! My sleep had been disturbed by the sound of gators fighting! I wouldn't have dozed off again so easily, if I had known what was making all that noise.

I was now only a day or so from Gainesville, and was just thinking how well my bike was running and how wrong the motorcycle shop guys had been, when the engine suddenly quit. I coasted to the side of the road, and kicked the starter a few times, but, no luck.

After checking gas, spark plug wires, and everything else I could think of, I finally took off a side cover, to find a wire hanging down: vibration or wind had broken it off. The problem now was that there was no way to re-connect the wire to the small spot of solder that was supposed to hold it in place, except by re-soldering. Stuck on the side of the road in Middle-of-Nowhere, Georgia, I couldn't see how I was going to be able to fix this problem.

Suddenly an idea occurred to me. I took a walk along the shoulder of the road and, within a few yards, came across just what I needed, a piece of scrap wire lying in the dirt. I twisted the bare end of the broken wire to the stripped middle of the scrap wire and then tied it to the bike in a way that the bare wire section made contact with the solder spot. I kicked the engine over, and away she went. My side-of-the-road repair worked so well that it got me all the way to my destination in Florida.

After a week seeing the sights in Gainesville, Jonathon and I were ready to hit the road north. We took a westerly route and rode up through the American south on a recently-opened section of the Blue Ridge Mountain Skyway, a beautiful ride through a gorgeous and, until recently, almost-inaccessible part of the country.

On our second day out, we were cruising through a rural part of Georgia close to the Alabama border when we passed a car with a flat tire. Four women, who looked to be dressed for church, were standing by the open trunk, obviously trying to figure out how to change the tire.

We turned around and went back to see if we could help. When we got off our bikes, one of the women immediately announced that their husbands were fishing in a stream nearby and would be right back any minute. It seemed a little odd to me that their husbands would leave them in their good

## Two Ferries Out

clothes to change the tire, but I said "That's OK, we don't mind doing it", and took the tire iron she was holding out of her hand.

By the time we got the tire changed, the husbands still hadn't returned. The women thanked us and we left.

It wasn't until years later, when I was thinking about this incident, that I finally realized what was going on. The four women were black, we were in an area of the south where just a few years before and a few miles away in Birmingham and Montgomery, Alabama, race riots and anti-segregation demonstrations had taken place. When two white guys on motorcycles pulled up to their disabled car, I'm sure we must have looked like their worst nightmare. There were no husbands nearby: that was just a story to scare us off.

I probably came within a hair's breadth of getting that tire iron upside the head. But being a naïve guy from Brier Island, I was oblivious to all that at the time, I just saw some people who needed help and lent a hand.

The rest of the trip involved a two-thousand-mile detour to Cincinnati, Ohio to see a girl who had visited Brier Island for three days the previous summer (that tenuous connection), getting frisked at the border, rear-ending a taxi in Toronto because I was distracted by a pretty girl on the sidewalk, and getting peppered by flying ants while driving all night through Vermont to catch the Bar Harbour ferry back home.

**Ben Robicheau**

Except for the broken wire, my bike ran perfectly throughout the whole trip. I sold it a month later to someone in Digby. He came to Westport to pick it up, and it died at Lake Midway on the way back.

I guess the bike shop guys from Yarmouth were right after all; they just had their timing off a bit.

*The bike I rode to Florida.*

## 41: Strawberry fields forever

In the month of August, in the summer of 1969, some of us envious Brier Island teenagers watched in awe as half a million people made their way to Max Yasgur's farm in upstate New York to attend the Woodstock Music and Art Fair. This concert became renowned around the world as the largest music festival ever held. Today, most people know about Woodstock and its place in popular music history. What many people do not know however, is that another music festival, "a second Woodstock" took place in Canada one year later.

John Lennon originally put forward the idea in 1969, while he and Yoko Ono were in Montreal doing their famous Bed-In For Peace. He suggested holding an event to be called *The Toronto Music and Peace Festival* at Mosport Motor Park, a 500-acre auto-racing venue near Bowmanville, about an hour east of Toronto. The R.C.M.P. were keeping an eye on Lennon due to a drug conviction he had received in the U.S. a year before, and they made a concerted effort to influence locals against the idea of a Lennon-connected event by showing them film of nudity, violence, and drug use at U.S. musical events. This had the desired effect: people living near the park protested to authorities, who denied the necessary permits.

By this time, the Canadian promoters of the concert had already sold thousands of tickets, and invested a year's worth of money and effort in the venture. They felt they had no choice but to go ahead with the show, so the venue moved to a strawberry farm near Shediac, New Brunswick. Lennon, preoccupied with personal projects and the break-up of the Beatles, had dropped out of the venture, and the concert was renamed *Strawberry Fields – An International Carnival of Sound and Freedom*.

But once again, permits were denied when locals were scared off by the potential of being inundated by hundreds of thousands of "hippies", and quickly passed their own restrictive laws. As much as I would have loved to attend a real rock concert this close to home, this cancellation might have been for the best. There had been a rumour floating around that there was a plan to set up a stage on the Bay of Fundy shore and hold some of the performances there when the tide was out, with the audience gathered on the sand flats. Given the speed at which the twice-a-day tidal waters rise and fall in that area, concertgoers were most likely saved from a mass drowning when the location was abandoned, and the festival moved back to Ontario in its never-ending search for a home.

After a brief and futile attempt to locate in London, Ontario, the promoters came full circle and settled once again on Mosport Park. By this time they were well aware that a huge rock festival was not everyone's idea of a good neighbour, so they tried to keep things under wraps. To rent the facility without raising alarm bells, they disguised it as an automotive event by advertising the week-end as a motorcycle race with "added entertainment".

I had been in Toronto for a week or so, checking out Fall courses at Seneca College. On Friday morning of the festival weekend I was out on Highway 401, hitching home to Nova Scotia, when three guys in a '57 Chevy with Maryland plates pulled up and asked if I knew where Mosport was.

I had been following the story of the wandering rock concert, and the last I had heard was that the Attorney General for Ontario had brought an injunction application to prohibit the festival from taking place. I told them that I knew where Mosport was, but wasn't sure if the concert was on. They said if I came with them to show the way, and there was no concert, they would drive me to Nova Scotia. So I got in the car.

As we approached Mosport, it became obvious that the show was indeed going ahead. The roads were lined with cars and clogged with people walking towards the main gate. Since I had neither a ticket nor the spare money to buy one (it was $15 for the week-end), I got out of the car with the intention of heading back to the highway.

As I walked along the edge of the park, I noticed a line of people snaking into the bushes. I quickly took a place in line and within a few minutes was through a hole in the fence and inside the park.

The first thing I saw was a girl disappearing into the ground! It turned out that she had stepped into a hole hidden by the tall grass. I helped her out, and she introduced herself as Anne, from Texas.

Although the promoters had sold the event as a race in Canada, they had advertised it as a rock concert south of the border. As a result, Americans had bought a large percentage of the tickets, and many of them had spent the last few days wandering back and forth from Ontario to New Brunswick to Ontario in a confused attempt to catch up with the latest incarnation of the festival. When border officials noticed thousands of teenagers suddenly trying to flood north into Canada, some with nothing more than a pair of concert tickets, a few dollars, and a bag of groceries to last them the week-end, they turned them back by the hundreds. Still, most managed to find an alternate route over the border.

Anne and I made our way across the race track to the infield area, where there was a stage with a massive sound system. The ground in front of the stage was packed with people who had staked out their area with a sleeping bag or blanket. Most of them would spend the next three days in this same tiny spot. I found an empty patch of ground next to the fence, and marked out my own little space.

The performers for the week-end included Procol Harum, Ten Years After, Eric Burdon & War, Grand Funk Railroad, Sly & the Family Stone, Jethro Tull,

# Two Ferries Out

Mountain, Crowbar, Luke and The Apostles, The Youngbloods, Melanie, Delaney and Bonnie, Leonard Cohen, Jose Feliciano and a little-known-at-the-time performer named Alice Cooper, maybe a female folk singer?

I spent the next three days in the middle of a sea of between 75,000 and 100,000 people. The bands took the stage in the late afternoon, and went on into the early morning hours. We spent the time between performances attempting to get some sleep, trying to find a Port-A-Potty fit for human use, or foraging for food.

Word quickly spread throughout the surrounding area that a full-scale rock concert was in progress, and hundreds of local kids began showing up without tickets, trying to gain admission. Things got so confusing and hectic that by noon Saturday, the organizers finally just threw open the gates, and people could come and go as they pleased.

The only store nearby was inundated with hungry, thirsty concert-goers, and was quickly stripped bare of anything that could be remotely considered food or drink. Water trucks were brought in, and local entrepreneurs arrived with everything from toilet paper to a tractor-trailer full of watermelons. There was a medical tent, and members of a local commune were handing out free oranges, sandwiches, and soup to those who had run out of money.

On Saturday afternoon, the motorcycle race, the supposed reason for the gathering, took place. It was a total disaster. The official motorcycle racing organization that was supposed to oversee the event had pulled out when they realized they had been duped into serving as a front for a rock concert. A few of the riders agreed to go ahead and stage an unofficial race anyway.

It did not go well.

Without course officials to keep order, people were sitting and standing in dangerous spots and wandering across the track at random, oblivious to the bikes. The race had to be started and stopped several times, the PA announcer kept telling people to stay off the course. It looked like someone could easily get killed. Finally some of the concert-goers stepped in as voluntary course marshals, trying to control the spectators and warn the racers of obstacles ahead. After forty minutes or so of this erratic, stop-and-go "racing", they cancelled the race for everyone's safety.

I found out years later, when talking to one of the racers, that they were paid $50 each and told, "no racing, just complete three laps of the track". All the organizers wanted was to meet their obligation by appearing to hold a race. The guy I talked to said he had a leisurely ride around the course, and had the unique racing experience of being greeted at the hairpin turn by several naked people waving at him. He just waved back and continued on.

Alice Cooper played late Saturday night. Definitely not a folk singer, he put on an incredible light and sound show that had the audience amazed and mesmerized. The concert was supposed to end Sunday

## Two Ferries Out

night, but the schedule had long since gone out the window, and the last act took the stage early Monday morning.

By now, most of the audience had left. Those of us remaining slowly packed up our gear just as the sun was coming up and headed for the exits with "I Want To Take You Higher" ringing in our ears.

The last act, Sly & the Family Stone, closed the show with what those of us still there to see it believed was the best performance of the weekend.

Anne had gone off to find the friends she had come with, and I, along with thousands of others, made my way back to the Trans Canada, where I caught a ride with some Americans who were headed east to the Thousand Islands Bridge border crossing. A couple of miles from the bridge, traffic came to a complete stop; it was backed up from the border out to the 401 highway.

I got out, and caught a ride with a car that had just come across the bridge; the driver said that American border guards were disassembling cars going into the States on the side of the road, probably looking for drugs. He said people waiting on the bridge just before the border station were getting out of their cars and tossing some suspicious-looking stuff into the St Lawrence River below.

A couple of days later, I was back home, at work in the poolroom I had been running all summer, when, to my astonishment, in walked Anne from Texas!

**Ben Robicheau**

She had tried to convince her friends to head east, but they decided to go west instead, so she set out on her own. All she knew about me was my first name, that I lived on an island in Nova Scotia, and that I had seven sisters; she figured that, working with this wealth of information, I wouldn't be too hard to find.

Having made it to Halifax, she was sitting on the sidewalk by the Public Gardens fence, trying to figure out what to do next, when a police officer approached her. He met her explanation of what she was doing, and who she was looking for, with a blank stare; but the officer had a new recruit with him who thought her description sounded a lot like a guy named Benny whom he had gone to school with in Digby.

When she got to Digby, someone sent her to the only Benny they knew, an old fellow who had a garage in Barton, just outside of town. She quickly figured out that this was not the right guy, but again, luck was on her side. Someone from the Islands happened to be at the garage, heard her story, and headed her in the right direction.

Someone I met briefly a thousand miles away, with only very basic information about me, comes to the province and, by talking to a few random people, is able to track me down! I'm not sure that 'he lives on an island and has seven sisters' was a major clue that helped her find me, but somehow it worked.

## 42: A whale of a tale

As in most small communities, the job options on Brier Island are rather limited. If your interests do not run to something connected to the sea or the tourism industry, you must seek opportunities further afield. Unfortunately, this is a route many of the young people of the Island have had to take, and I was one of them.

I ended up working at the Ontario Science Centre in Toronto, But even here, in the biggest city in Canada, a little bit of Brier Island has followed me. If you ever happen to find yourself in the Living Earth section of the Ontario Science Centre, be sure to look up, way, way up. You will see, suspended from the ceiling, the skeleton of a sixty-foot Fin whale. You might well wonder how this former Bay of Fundy denizen came to reside in a city so far from the sea.

In the summer of 1977, I made my annual trek back east for my summer vacation. While I was home, a dead whale washed up on Long Island, the first one to come ashore in several years.

When I got back to Toronto, I casually mentioned the whale to one of the Science Centre staff, who excitedly informed me that they were looking for a whale skeleton to exhibit.

At his request, I immediately phoned my father, only to learn that the whale in question had drifted out to sea again. I asked him to let me know if another whale happened to come ashore, assuming it might be a few more years before another one turned up.

Two weeks later, my father called me to report that he had a whale for me if I was still interested.

At the time, Dr. Peter Beamish, a biologist with the Bedford Institute of Oceanography, had a sideline of running nature treks for kids. While camping near Pond Cove, he had come across a dead Fin whale on the east side of Point D' Field.

While Peter and his group secured the whale so that this one wouldn't escape, I went to see how serious the Science Centre really was about this whole whale thing.

It turned out they were very serious. Within twenty-four hours, I was on a plane to Nova Scotia with Lorraine Dumoulin. Lorraine had dissected frogs while earning her biology degree, and was the closest thing the Science Centre had to an expert on whale skinning. Although I had estimated it would take at least a couple of weeks to do the job, we had just one week to complete our project.

Arriving in Halifax, we went to see Dr. Beamish for advice on the easiest and fastest way to extract the skeleton from a whale. Peter had an extensive interest in whales, and had spent years studying the whaling industry, acquiring information and equipment from the many whale-processing stations that used to exist along the Atlantic coast.

One of the artifacts he had in his office was a flensing knife, which looked a bit like a hockey stick, with a long wooden handle, and a dangerous-looking curved, eighteen-inch metal blade. This was the main tool whalers used to cut through the thick layers of blubber. In Dr. Beamish's opinion, our job would be nearly impossible without it. Since this knife was both an antique and a collector's item, he didn't want to let it go; but he recommended a "metal artist" in Bear River who could build us a couple of new ones.

Arriving in Westport armed with two surprisingly-accurate replicas of the whale skinner's basic tool, we added to our arsenal two splitting knives, a bucksaw, and a couple of the biggest carving knives we could find. We also added to our group Greg Hannah, a New York artist who spends summers on the island; his friend Lenny; and my sister Janet.

The five of us gathered our gear and headed down Pond Cove Road to see what exactly we had gotten ourselves into.

The whale, a sixty-foot mass of black and white blubber with a gaping hole in the middle where sharks had been ripping at it, nearly filled the small cove. Cutting away all those tons of flesh and pulling out the ribs, vertebrae, jaw bones, skull and numerous other smaller bones seemed like an impossible task, especially since none of us really had any idea what we were doing.

By the second day, guided by a book on whale biology that Lorraine had luckily thought to bring along, we were beginning to make some headway, when Lenny cut through his rubber boot with one of the razor-sharp flensing knives, and sliced a deep gash into the side of his foot.

Janet took him over to Dr. Stokes in Freeport, who unfortunately was out of anaesthetic to freeze the wound. Instead, he gave Lenny a rolled-up towel to bite on while he stitched the wound up.

According to fishermen on the island, the carcass had been drifting around for nearly a month, possibly the victim of a collision with a large ship. By the time it reached shore, it was starting to decompose, and lying on the beach in the August sun sped up the process considerably. By the time we got to it, it was a slowly decomposing mass of greasy flesh, emitting a smell that was quite noticeable, but not yet unbearable.

As the week went on, and disassembly of the creature advanced, the odour grew gradually worse; but because we were around it all day, we adjusted to the smell and didn't realize how bad it was getting.

We did notice that the group that came down every day to observe and take pictures stood farther and farther back as each day passed. How ripe we were getting was finally brought home to us at noon on the third day, when we went to my father's store to get some lunch, as we had been doing every day. On this day, Dad met us at the door with a can of air freshener in his hand, and told us to stay outside, he'd bring our lunch out to us.

## Two Ferries Out

Janet says she remembers Dubie Frost stopping to discuss the whale, but backing up further and further as he talked to us.

Aside from the foot episode, things were going surprisingly well on the disassembly. Every time the tide came up, it covered the whale and carried away most of the large slabs of blubber we had cut off. We were able to pull some ribs out of the damaged midsection, and were gradually building up a stockpile of bits and pieces above the high-water mark. We built skids out of driftwood, and used a four-wheel-drive truck to haul some of the larger sections up the beach, once we had separated them from the carcass.

By the end of the week, just as the smell was finally getting to be too much for even us to bear, we were relieved, and as amazed as everyone else, to see that we had actually succeeded in collecting a pile of bones that comprised a complete whale skeleton. We had everything from the fifteen-foot jaw bones to the nickel-coin-sized ear bones that we had managed to dig out of the massive skull. The only things missing were a couple of ribs that sharks had made off with before the carcass reached shore.

Now all we had to do was get this smelly mess to Toronto.

The man for the job was Danny Kenney. He had to build an extension onto one of his trucks to fit everything in, but he managed to get it all loaded, packed in hay, and covered with a tarp. He decided to take the U.S. route to Ontario, and here his extensive experience in travelling back and forth across the border came in handy.

Somehow, he was able to cross into the States with a minimum of trouble, and then back out again, carrying a stinking, dripping load of whalebones and decaying blubber. Granted, this was well before events in the U.S. caused a tightening of restrictions at the border; but even so, this was quite a feat.

Arriving in Toronto the evening before he was scheduled to deliver his load, Danny decided to spend the night at his sister's house. She lived in a nice neighbourhood on the outskirts of the city, and while happy to see her brother, for some reason she wasn't thrilled about having his truck and its fragrant load parked in her driveway. Danny had to go find a gas station that was willing to let him park his truck overnight, I believe he even had to pay them to take it.

Now that we had the whale, what did we do with it? There was still meat attached to many of the bones, so we unloaded them straight from the truck and buried them in the ground. The theory was that bugs in the soil would clean the flesh from the bones.

Two years later, we dug the bones up, and then dropped them into Lake Ontario. Whale bones are full of oil which will continue to ooze out for years. If you sink the bones deep enough, the water pressure forces the oil out.

After the bones spent a couple of years in the lake, and after many jokes about whales in Lake Ontario, we finally brought them to the Science Centre. There they spent another year on the roof, drying and bleaching in the sun. Finally, they were steam-cleaned and prepared for assembly.

*Me and my whale*

By the spring of 1984, the public finally got to see the bones on display. They were spread out in the Great Hall, part of the main entrance to the Science Centre, where an expert who usually reconstructs dinosaur skeletons carefully sorted and assembled them. Over the next few months, thousands of visitors got to see the Bay of Fundy behemoth take shape.

Upon completion, the skeleton was carefully moved to the Living Earth section and suspended from the ceiling, finally ending its long journey from the sea.

**Ben Robicheau**

Now, many years and many miles from the Fundy shores, Fundy The Whale is one of the Science Centre's most popular exhibits, impressing and educating thousands of school children every year.

## 43: Eastward bound

After leaving Brier Island to go to school, and after that, to work, I made it a habit to come home for Christmas. It was just an overnight, twenty-two-hour drive from Toronto to Halifax, if I only stopped for gas and something to eat. The trip home for Christmas, family gatherings or summer vacation is a ritual that many Islanders perform on a regular basis. Whether you are coming from somewhere else in Nova Scotia, across Canada or from the other side of the world, you're on a journey that ends with a ferry ride.

Over the years, I've travelled between Ontario and Nova Scotia by plane, train, bus, truck, car, motorcycle and thumb. I've done the trip driving all night by myself, accompanied by other Islanders, and with newcomers to the Islands who didn't really believe my stories about where I grew up until I showed them over the place in person.

The drive these days is better than it used to be. From where I live now in Hamilton to Halifax it's all divided highway, except for a short section of good-quality two-lane road near the Quebec-New Brunswick border. In comparison, my first trips to visit relatives in Ontario were before the Trans-Canada was finished, and the road through Quebec was a time-consuming stop-and-go route along the St.

Lawrence River, through numerous little towns with big churches all named Saint something-or-other.

Janet Morton's mother is from the Island and she still has relatives here. Her family was in the military and lived for many years in Ontario, so the yearly trip home is burned into her memory.

> *Long before the main highways, (no 401 in Ontario) the 20 and 40 through Quebec and the newer one down through northern New Brunswick, we travelled that path every summer from Ontario to Nova Scotia. We didn't measure it in hours, but in days, Dad was the only driver and I still don't know how he ever survived those drives with us monsters in the car.*
>
> *Sometimes there was an extra child to drop off in Bear River or another quiet place. Many people where we lived on the base were from the Maritimes, and would send their children, with whoever would take them, to visit families in the east.*
>
> *I remember the heat, the windows open trying to get relief, the noise! Most of it from us kids. Stopping beside the highway, not at a fancy rest stop, for warm drinks and mushy sandwiches and, if we were lucky, a stream to cool off in. The wet bathing suits hanging on the aerial to dry while we drove, broken-up radio stations, the games we came up with to*

## Two Ferries Out

*play. Counting licence plates?? I can't even see them now; they all look the same.*

*Richard preferred the back window-seat, but I'm not sure how he could stand the heat, Barry liked to watch the road, and I just wanted to get there! We won't even get into car breakdowns, repairs, and time involved in that. Did I mention we tented both ways? Those old canvas tents can get pretty crowded and hot at night! I am surprised my mother survived all those trips.*

My first December in Ontario, I was looking for an economical way to get home for Christmas when my Aunt Minnie came up with a solution. Having worked for a car rental company, she knew that they had cars that needed to be moved to different locations around the country and even paid people to drive them from place to place. She made a call, and sure enough, there was a car in Toronto, waiting to be delivered to Saint John, New Brunswick.

I picked it up after school, and headed east in a brand-new, straight-from-the-factory, 1970 Plymouth Duster with summer tires and power steering.

An O.P.P. officer stopped me before I had even left the city. His attention had been drawn by my unsteady driving and the fact that the car had no plates. After my explanation that I was just getting used to the power steering, and a thorough examination of the temporary permit in the side window, he let me go with the observation that it was December and I really should have winter tires on. I wasn't worried about the tires because the roads were clear and there was no sign of snow.

Four hours later, I was in the middle of a howling blizzard, sitting at a dead stop in a miles-long line of traffic. After three hours of sitting, idling, and watching the gas gauge steadily sink towards "empty", I took a chance, and plowed my way into the tracks that had been left by several four-wheel-drive vehicles that had passed us by.

Despite the lack of snow tires, I was able to keep moving, and eventually reached the head of the line to see what had been holding things up all this while: a transport truck uselessly spinning its wheels.

As I continued eastward, the storm lessened, and by the time I hit New Brunswick, the road was mostly bare, with just a thin layer of wet snow at the edges. The sun was coming up, and I was the only car on the road. I had to make up for lost time if I was going to catch the morning ferry to Digby.

I was doing close to one hundred miles per hour when I wandered slightly out of my cleared lane and into the slush at the edge of the pavement. The car fishtailed to the right, then swung left, then right again, making a bigger arc each time. I knew I was going to lose control, and figured it would be better if I slid towards the road than the ditch. When the car slid left again, I slammed on the brakes. This threw me into a couple of hair-raising and anxiety-

## Two Ferries Out

producing three-hundred-and-sixty-degree spins, and I finally came to rest on the other side of the luckily-deserted road, facing in the opposite direction, white-knuckled and shaking, but unscathed.

I made the ferry okay, but I never told my aunt how close I came to wiping out that brand-new Duster.

Just before Christmas a year later, I got a phone call from fellow-Islander Peggy Thompson. She was on her way home from British Columbia and wanted to know if I could give her a lift east from Toronto. As it happened, I had just become the proud owner of a ten-year-old VW Beetle with 200,000 miles on it, and I was glad to have the company.

When we set out, the weather was good, but by the time we hit Montreal, it was snowing and extremely cold. The Beetle's heating system was not known as being a great heat-producer at the best of times, and asking it to compete with a Quebec winter was just asking for trouble. Our breath froze on the inside of the windshield to the extent that we had to use an ice scraper on the inside of the glass to see where we were going, and Peggy had to periodically reach out the window to clear snow off the windshield that the wipers couldn't get.

After a long, cold night, we finally made it to the Digby ferry, crossed the Bay and happily started down the Neck. We were almost home! Then we ran into a problem that is familiar to every Islander, as Peggy tells it:

**Ben Robicheau**

> *After a very long trip, we ventured down Digby Neck behind the snowplow...only to get to East Ferry and find that the ferry wasn't crossing! I had come all the way from Prince George...hit an avalanche in Rogers Pass in the Rockies, driven frozen through Quebec to New Brunswick, gotten seasick crossing the Bay of Fundy, risked my neck on Digby Neck only to find the FRIGGIN' FERRY WASN'T CROSSING!!!!!*

Many of my early trips were in the company of fellow Islander Herb Barnaby, who was going to university in Ontario. One trip he likes to remind me about is when I misjudged how far I could go on a tank of gas, and ran out just as we were going up a hill. Herb was just envisioning us freezing to death in the dark beside the highway when, with our last bit of momentum, we slowly crested the hill to see a gas station on the other side. We were able to coast most of the way, although Herb and my sister Janet did have to get out and push the car the last fifty feet to the pumps.

On another occasion, I had Herb and his brother Rodney, as well as Rodney's German Shepherd, Shamus, all crammed into the cab of my Toyota truck. With the four of us in such close quarters, the windshield fogged up and froze, to the extent that we only had a small hole to see out of. Herb says he remembers changing lanes as we went through Montreal with no idea if anyone was beside us be-

## Two Ferries Out

cause he could hardly see out the front, and the side windows were totally iced up.

When we finally got to New Brunswick, the road from Fredericton to Saint John was a glare of ice, and we were reduced to a crawl. As usual, we were pressed for time to make the Digby boat, and at our current rate we were probably going to miss it.

Luckily, in New Brunswick you couldn't go far without seeing pulpwood stacked on the side of the road. One of these piles conveniently appeared now, so I stopped, tossed a couple of logs into the back of the truck and, with the added weight providing traction, we made the ferry on time.

I hadn't been thrilled about taking a dog with us, but Shamus turned out to be an excellent traveller. Though I don't know where he found the room in that small truck, he lay curled up on the cab floor for the whole trip.

The only sign of complaint I saw from him was when we had to leave him in the truck on the Digby ferry. I don't know if it was out of boredom or in protest at being left alone, but he passed the two-hour trip by chewing on the wooden gearshift knob that I had made in Herbie Thurber's high school woodworking class. I was able to sand out most of the tooth marks, but a few remain to this day as a memento of the trip.

Some wise person once said, "You can't go home again," but it seems that, with a bit of perseverance, you can. A good set of snow tires helps a lot, too.

**Ben Robicheau**

## 44: On being an Islander

The word "island" comes from the Latin "insula", which is the root of the word "isolation". Growing up in Westport, I often had the feeling of being in a place separate from the rest of the world, which is, I guess, not all that surprising. Being stuck two ferries out into the ocean, in a time well before the advent of the internet, cheap long distance, cell phones, satellite, and all the many ways in which we now communicate with each other, I guess it was only natural that one would tend to feel a little isolated and removed from the mainstream of society.

Of course, this wasn't necessarily a bad thing. During much of my childhood, there was a "cold war" going on, which consisted mainly of the two "Superpowers" of the world, the United States and the U.S.S.R, threatening to blow each other up. There was constant talk of The Arms Race, Intercontinental Ballistic Missiles, Nuclear Winter, and a comforting and reassuring Defence Department strategy called Mutually Assured Destruction.

Somehow, despite being constantly bombarded with news of such events as The Bay of Pigs, U.S. pilot Francis Gary Powers being shot down in his C.I.A. spy plane over Russia, and U.S. troops landing in Da Nang, the fact that I lived on a militarily-insignificant speck in the ocean gave me, for the most part, a feeling that, whatever happened in the rest of the world, I was safe here. This feeling was occasionally disrupted by a sense of unease when I remembered that one of the major players in this battle for world dominance existed only a few miles away across the Gulf of Maine, and that one of the prime targets in any nuclear attack would surely be New York City. There was nothing between the two islands, Manhattan and Brier, but open water, nothing at all to deflect the effects of a nuclear blast.

Luckily, these negative thoughts were fleeting; as far as I could tell, no one else on the Island shared my worries. Or if they did, they kept it to themselves.

It was around this time that I began to become aware that Island people are a special breed. As a child, I didn't know that it takes a certain temperament to be able to live on an island. To me, there wasn't anything out of the ordinary about the place where I lived. It didn't seem at all unusual that our daily travels were restricted by the salt water that surrounded us, that we couldn't even consider leaving the Island after dark, and if we were off the Island, had to always make sure we headed back in time to catch the last ferry home.

The fact that we had to cross not one, but two passages on small wooden scows to get to the mainland, and that sometimes we couldn't leave the island at all due to bad weather, mechanical breakdown, or just because the ferryman didn't feel like taking you right now, was no big deal. I assumed that everyone, not just those who lived and worked on the sea,

## Two Ferries Out

listened faithfully to the radio for the weather report known locally as "the Probs", and planned the next twenty-four hours according to the probable weather conditions.

As I got older, I began to notice that not everyone was entirely comfortable with Island life. For instance, there was the travelling salesman who used to visit my father's store every couple of months. He always seemed kind of jumpy and nervous, and in a big hurry to get going. Every few minutes he would check to make sure the ferry was still crossing, and ask exactly where it was. He always appeared relieved when business was finally completed and he could escape back across the passage. He acted as if he was expecting the island to spring a leak and sink under him at any moment.

In the sixties, I attended school in Kentville and boarded with a family in town. Upon hearing where I was from, the man of the house launched into a story about a work trip he had made to Digby County a dozen years earlier. As he remembered it, he took a primitive barge to a tiny, sparsely populated island far off the coast. He was put up for the night in one of the few crude houses in the village, but got very little sleep because the barren, rocky island was only a couple of feet above the high-water mark, and he lay awake all night, worrying that the huge waves continuously pounding on the shore just outside his bedroom window might roll right over the whole settlement and sweep it out to sea.

**Ben Robicheau**

Trying to figure out what rock or ledge he had spent the night on, I asked a few more questions and was astounded to realize that he was talking about Brier Island. I tried to convince him that things couldn't really have been the way he described, but he was adamant that this was an accurate memory of one of the most terrifying experiences of his life.

Even only forty miles away in Digby, there were people who didn't seem to know or care all that much about the goings-on down Digby Neck. If you mentioned you were from the Islands, some people would profess to have never heard of the place, or worse yet, would act as if you had just confessed to being a resident of Dogpatch! Some considered Digby Neck and The Islands to be a wild and dangerous area, populated by a bunch of in-bred, moonshine-swilling, backwoods hillbillies, that got worse the farther down the Neck you went. People would proudly tell you that they had never been down The Neck, refusing to believe that there could possibly be anything down there that would make it worth the long drive and risky ocean crossings.

My mother once met a couple of tourists in Digby and invited them to visit Westport, but warned them that since it was a windy day, the ferry crossing might be a bit rough. They replied that they loved out-of-the-way places, and rough water was not a problem for them. They said they were famous among their cottage friends for being the only ones daring enough to take their boat out on the lake in choppy weather. Later that day, Mom happened to be

## Two Ferries Out

sitting in the line-up at East Ferry when she saw their car come down the hill. They took one look at the whitecaps in the harbour, and the flying spray as the ferry bucked its way across Petite Passage, then made a quick U-turn and headed back up the hill. I guess the Bay of Fundy gets a bit rougher than their cottage lake!

During the fifties, sixties, and even into the seventies, I don't remember many people visiting the Islands. You could sometimes go for weeks on end without seeing a strange face. Oh sure, there were those who regularly came down on business and others who had relatives to visit, but actual tourists were few and far between. Most of the scattered few who did come were of the "adventure tourist" type. If you asked them how they decided to visit the Islands, they would usually tell you that they just looked on the map for the most isolated and out-of-the-way, but still accessible, place they could find.

Then, of course, there was the occasional accidental tourist, like the couple who, after driving around the Island a couple of times, asked where the Bar Harbour ferry docked. Apparently, they hadn't looked at a map at all; they were on their way to Yarmouth, but drove down the wrong side of St. Mary's Bay!

For us kids, it always piqued our interest if a car with out-of-province plates drove off the ferry. And if it had U.S. plates, that seemed even more exotic! I can remember being a teenager with a carload of friends, following strange vehicles around the Island, trying to figure out if we knew who they were and, if not, why in the world they had come here. Looking back on it now, we must have made some people kind of nervous. Maybe that's one reason we didn't get more visitors!

By the late seventies, things began to change. Our little corner of the world that had been mostly overlooked and left behind finally started to get a bit of attention.

Ironically, the things that many now found appealing about the area were pretty much the same things that people had looked down on us for a few years earlier. Our life-style was no longer "boring" but "peaceful"; instead of being "in the boonies" we were now a place where people could "get away from it all". The lack of big-city hustle-and-bustle was now an asset rather than a detriment. As personal contact with the natural world got further and further out of reach for more and more people, they started to seek out places where it was still possible to partake in activities that would get them back in touch with The Great Outdoors.

Today, a mention that you're from the Islands can usually get you a positive response almost anywhere in Nova Scotia. Many people have been down the Neck whale-watching, camping, bird-watching, hiking, or just for a scenic drive (if the fog isn't in). The Island's renown has even spread across the country and around the world.

In the early two thousands, we moved to Hamilton, Ontario, where my wife Randi worked in a hospital. While chatting with a staff member, Randi mentioned that she had moved here from Nova Scotia. Her new colleague replied that she loved Nova Scotia; several years ago, she had vacationed there as a newly-wed and had wonderful memories of her visit to a lovely little island in the Bay of Fundy. You guessed it: she had spent her honeymoon camping at Pond Cove!

My sister-in-law lived in France for a while. One evening, she was out for dinner, when out of the hubbub of conversation around her, the words "Nova Scotia" happened to come to her ear. The couple at a nearby table were discussing their favourite travel experiences, and she was surprised to hear the woman state to her companion that, of all the places she had visited, she thought the most beautiful was a little place called Brier Island!

What are the odds that two people chatting in Ontario, or two strangers who happened to sit near each other in a restaurant in Paris, would discover they had a connection to Brier Island? Over the course of a few decades, the Islands have gone from a mysterious, isolated area that few people wanted to visit, to a unique tourist destination being discussed in the cafes of Paris!

It's now been more than fifty years since I've lived on Brier Island, but I return as often as I can. I don't believe I've ever let more than a year elapse between visits, and I still consider myself an Islander. There is a part of my brain that is permanently dedicated to keeping track of the ferry schedule and calculating what time I have to leave wherever I am in order to catch the next crossing. Traffic noise keeps me awake at night, but I can sleep through the droning of a foghorn, no problem, even the new electronic ones!

Some things are just ingrained, they stick with you no matter how long you've been away.

## 45: Two ferries out

Whenever I attempt to describe my childhood to strangers, I find myself telling them that I grew up on an island "two ferries out" from the mainland. This is often met with a blank stare, so I then have to go into more detail, explaining that, to reach this island, you have to first take a ferry from the mainland to Long Island, then drive the length of that island to the second ferry, which takes you to Brier Island. So, two ferries out.

The island ferries are not like most other ferries in the province. They are not an alternate route to save a long drive around, like the LaHave River ferry, or a scenic commuting choice like the Halifax-Dartmouth ferries. The Island ferries are not a quaint travel option: they are the only option. The only way on or off the islands is over water; all goods and services arrive by ferry. Need a doctor, dentist, or hairdresser? Need to take your pet to the vet? Need your broken eyeglasses replaced? It's all on the other side of the ferry.

I've often wondered why island residents have to pay to use the ferry. It's not like they have a choice: these ferries are an integral part of the highway system. Why do they have to pay extra to access the rest of the province? I'm sure people on the mainland would not be happy if a tollgate was placed at the end of their driveway and they had to pay to get to the public roads, yet this is the situation for Islanders. (In 2021 I was pleased to hear that the provincial government finally saw the error of its ways, and abolished the fees on all ferries.)

The ferries today are government owned and operated, but that has not always been the case. Back in the early days, when most people along the coast travelled by boat, the ferry was basically a raft propelled by oars and sails, only brought out by the owner on the rare occasion that something too large to be transported in a dory or fishing boat needed to be carried across the passage and landed on the beach.

*Westport Ferry – early forties.*

## Two Ferries Out

The arrival of the automobile brought with it improved roads, more travel, and a privately-operated regular ferry service. A barge propelled by a fishing boat replaced the raft, and could carry a couple of cars across the passage and land them at the new ferry ramps. These ferry services were private, locally-owned enterprises. For fifteen years, up until the early forties, Arthur Sullivan ran the Grand Passage ferry.

By the time I was old enough to pay attention to such things, from the mid-fifties on, Emerson 'Friday' Titus owned and ran the ferry. It still consisted of a purpose-built scow lashed to a boat, but the scow could carry up to six cars, and a stubbier, tug-style boat had replaced the fishing boat. The ferry did not run on any sort of set schedule; it just travelled back and forth as needed.

Over the years there were several different systems to alert the ferry if you were waiting on the other side. One was a very loud siren. You pushed the button and the ferryman could hear the siren blast on the other side of the harbour. I seem to recall that there was a code system: one blast if you were a pedestrian and only needed the boat, and two blasts if you were in a car and needed the scow. I'm sure the people who lived near the ferry slips loved this system.

Eventually, phone boxes mounted on a pole at the head of each slip replaced the sirens. Of course, if the ferry was not in, or the tide was low so the ferry was far away from the phone and it was a long walk up the slip, or the wind was blowing so they didn't hear the ring, the ferryman would not answer the call. Passersby or people working on the wharf got in the habit of answering the phone if they were nearby, and would relay the message to the guys on the ferry.

*Westport ferry - 1956.*

Although the government regulated the ferry service as far as safety and equipment went, it was a privately-owned business, subject to the decisions

## Two Ferries Out

and whims of the owner. The ferry scow did not cross after dark, so if you were driving, you had to leave your car on the other side until morning. You yourself could get home, because the boat itself usually made trips up until midnight; but these were infrequent and you might wait a long time for the ferry to arrive.

The crossings were really up to the decision of the owner. There might be many legitimate, and some not-so-legitimate, reasons why the ferry would not come get you. It might be too dark, too rough, too foggy, too windy, too late, or too few paying passengers to make it worthwhile. You might even get stranded just because the operator felt like taking some time off, I once heard the ferry captain refuse to make an evening crossing because he was about to go home and watch his favourite TV show, *Gunsmoke*.

In 1962, Islands Consolidated School opened in Freeport and the high school students from Westport began their daily trek across the passage to attend school. Foot passengers on the ferry had two choices: stand outside on the scow, or jump across the two-to-four-foot gap of open water between the scow and boat and take shelter in the cabin. The preferred option by far was to shelter in the cabin, especially if the weather was bad. Unfortunately, bad weather usually made the scow-to-boat transition a bit tricky. The boat was a moving target as it constantly moved in and out and up and down in relation to the scow. Stepping across the ever-changing gap from the scow deck to the narrow washboard of the boat was a challenge even on good days. On stormy, wet, icy, or snowy days it was downright dangerous. This was especially so for female students, who, until they rebelled against the rule, were not allowed by the school to wear pants, despite having to stand out on the wharf exposed to all kinds of weather, jump across open water, and occasionally climb up and down ladders.

As you can imagine, these less-than-ideal conditions made for a few unfortunate incidents. Over the years, countless text books, school bags, and lunch boxes were fished out of the gap between boat and scow, as well as two or three unlucky students. The situation became more and more untenable as more grades were eliminated at the Westport school and younger and younger students transferred to ICS.

Eventually the Westport school closed completely and all the students, from Primary to Grade Twelve, had to cross on the ferry. By now, the school board had decided that, instead of having five-year-olds walking up and down the ferry slips and competing with cars and trucks, it made more sense to send a school bus across on the ferry to pick up and transport the students. This was a relief to many of the parents, but resulted in the enforcement of what some thought was the ridiculous rule of students sitting in a bus on the ferry having to wear life jackets.

From its inception, the ferry had maintained the same basic form, a boat lashed to a scow. Although over time both the boat and scow enjoyed modest improvements in design, the basic style of the ferry service hadn't really changed in a hundred years.

Sometime around the beginning of the seventies, the provincial government began to take over the service. One of the first major changes they made was to get rid of the boat and make the scow self-propelled. They did this by modifying the steel scow that had been part of the boat-scow combination, adding engines, a wheel-house, and passenger accommodations along one side.

Since the scow had not been designed to carry this added weight, it resulted in a decidedly lopsided and slightly alarming appearance. Some locals began to take bets on how long it would stay afloat. During its retrofit, the scow had been painted yellow and named *Petite Passage II*, but locally it was known as *The Yellow Submarine*.

The Yellow Submarine was a prototype to see if this style of ferry would work in the strong currents and weather conditions of Grand Passage. At first, it didn't look too good. There were multiple equipment failures, an inadequate propulsion system had to be changed, design flaws that needed correction. There was a period when the ferry being rescued by the Coast Guard was almost a daily occurrence, and days of island residents being stranded while the broken-down-again ferry was tied up at the wharf.

But eventually, most of the bugs were worked out, and the information gained from the trials and tribulations of The Yellow Submarine went into the design of a new, purpose-built ferry, one with improved accommodations, better equipment and the ability to handle more and larger vehicles. It floated a lot straighter, too.

Today, the ferry service to the islands is much improved. The newest ferry, *Margaret's Justice*, runs twenty-four hours a day, can cross in almost any weather, runs on a set schedule, and can carry over twenty cars at a time; and there is a spare ferry available in case of break-down.

*Margaret's Justice - 2020*

This chapter about ferries was a last-minute addition. As I was preparing to send my collection of stories off to the publisher, I realized that, despite the name I had chosen for the book and casual mentions here and there, I had not dedicated much space to the ferries. At first, I could not believe that I had made such an oversight, but then I realized that it is a perfect demonstration of the effect Island life can have on a person, an effect that remains strong, even though I have not lived on the Island I still call 'home', for over fifty years.

The ferries were then, and still are today, so much a part of life on the Islands that, despite being essential to the existence of the Island communities, it is easy to overlook them. A constant background to life on Brier Island is the sound of the ferry crossing the passage, a sound that only registers with many residents when it is missing or off schedule.

Growing up on the Island, such things as seeing whales blowing from my living-room window, stopping to watch them breach up by Northern Light while out for a Sunday drive; the fact that we needed not one, not two, but three lighthouses to protect our small island from the treacherous waters that surrounded it; the need to negotiate not one, but two ferries to get on and off the island, were just unremarkable parts of everyday Island life.

Today, these are some of the things that attract hundreds of visitors every year to our unique little part of the world, only a ferry ride (or two) away!

**Ben Robicheau**

# Acknowledgements

I wrote these stories over a number of years, partly as a way of passing on to anyone who might be interested in a sense of what it was like to grow up in such a unique place and, to be truthful, partly so I would have a permanent record of my own memories before they all fade away.

I thank

> my wife, Randi, for her constant encouragement to record for posterity the stories I've been telling her over the last forty years so we can pass them on to our children and grandchildren.
> 
> My children, Sarah and Michael, and their spouses, Steven and Katherine, who actually seem interested when I tell them about things "back when I was a kid".
> 
> Felix, Charlie, and Lyla, my grandchildren, who, I hope will one day read this book and get a sense of where they come from and what helped make their Opa the person he is.

I would also like to thank

> Andy Moir and staff for allowing me to present these stories to a wider audience, and the readers of *Passages* who were entertained by my sometimes-faulty memories.
>
> And Brenda Thompson and Andrew Wetmore of Moose House Publications, for their interest and assistance in turning my stories into a book.

# About the author

Ben Robicheau is the co-author with Jim Prime of *Fish and Dicks: Case files from the Digby Neck & Island Fish-Gutting Service & Detective Agency* (also published by Moose House).

He also co-authored two award-winning plays with Jim for the King's Shorts Ten Minute Play competition at The King's Theatre in Annapolis Royal. For several years he was a regular contributor to the Digby Neck and Islands newsletter, *Passages*.

Ben lives in Hamilton, Ontario, but visits his parents and sisters on Brier Island as often as possible.

www.ingramcontent.com/pod-product-compliance
Lightning Source LLC
Chambersburg PA
CBHW071411070526
44578CB00003B/549